MW01479077

DISCOVER, DEVELOP & DEPLOY YOUR GIFTS

OLUGBEMISOLA OLABODE

Heart Beat PRODUCTIONS INC.

TABLE OF CONTENTS

A man's gift makes room for him, and brings him before great men.

Proverbs 18:16

On the right you will find what's called a QR Code. Using your smartphone, and a QR reader app. take a picture of the code and it will take you directly to my website at **discoveryourgift.net**

ACKNOWLEGEMENTS

I would like to thank the Almighty God for blessing me with this gift of writing and for being my God. Without him, I am nothing. Thank you Lord.

I would also like to thank my husband, David Olabode and children (Fikayomi, Feranmi, Fiyibomi and Divine) for all their support and encouragement at all times. Thanks for being there.

My next set of thanks goes to two ladies, my sister-in-law, Rali Macaulay, who God used to both challenge and encourage the gift of God in me. She was a person I knew who had numerous gifts. I did not however know she had books on the inside of her that she had been trying to write for a couple of years until she wrote her first series of books. I say this because she released about 4 books in a period of about 5 months. That really stirred me up. Thank you for challenging me to go higher.

The other lady that continually challenged me was Terri Savelle Foy. I have been listening to her for a good number of years and her messages have been such a blessing and inspiration to me. You can't listen to her and not be challenged. I want to say a big thank you for being a mentor and a big blessing to the body of Christ.

For Dr. Win Wachsmann and Dr. Carrie Wachsmann for coming into my life and helping me maneuver the "writing" waters. Without your help, I might not have been able to accomplish this feat. Thank you for everything.

To the members of RCCG, Jesus House Abbotsford for your continuous support through the years.

Lack of space limits me from mentioning other family and friends that have helped along the way. Thank you all.

INTRODUCTION

You have a gift; I have a gift! The woman on the street has a gift. The man in prison has a gift. We all have gifts that were placed in us when we were born. However, as much as it is good to know you have a gift, it is much more important to find out how that gift can be developed and put to use in your life and in your world.

You might be wondering, what do I mean by a "gift?" A gift here refers to a natural ability, talent or skill (flair, aptitude, facility, bent, ability, capacity and expertise). A gift refers to the ability or potential you were endowed with when you were created. No one was born empty; everyone was born with a gift or even multiple gifts. This gift could also refer to the skills you have been able to develop while you have been on this earth.

These gifts have a wide range. They could be creative such as dance, drama, choreography, creative arts, modeling, building, drawing, designing, sewing. They could be skills developed in a trade such as automobiles, construction, welding, woodworking, crocheting, knitting and hairdressing.

You could have an excellent fashion sense. These gifts could be skills such as leadership skills and organizational skills. (Do you have a strong attention to detail?)

They could be culinary skills (baking, catering, cooking), event planning. They could be communication skills (writing, teaching, speaking, coaching, training). They could be sales and marketing skills (which you need to effectively run a business). In this age of information technology, do you have proficient computer skills? (Web designing, info design, web marketing, media designing, a SEO specialty?) Do you have skills in TV, film or video?

Do you love photography? Do you have people skills? Do you have the gift of mercy, of helps, of listening, of compassion (Are you called to open up an orphanage or take prostitutes off the street)? I could go on and on. I however, have a question for you. Have you discovered your gift? If you have, what are you doing with it?

I am set to challenge you in this book. I am tired of seeing people let all God has put in them just go to waste… It's time to get up and begin to walk in your gifting. It's time to manifest, You are not waiting on God! God is waiting on you and your world is waiting too!

"For all creation, gazing eagerly as if with outstretched neck, is waiting and longing to see the manifestation of the sons of God."
Weymouth New Testament –Romans 8:19

As you read this book, I will encourage you to not just flip through the pages but rather to engage with it and ask yourself some questions. Questions that will lead you to discover your own gifts if you have not done so already. Questions such as: what gifts has God put in me? What do I love to do? What do I have the ability to do naturally? What do I have the skills to do that I am not doing presently?

We will not only be looking at your gifts, as you may have a couple of them, but we shall also be looking at how you can discover what your most dominant gifts are, and how you can use them to impact your world.

I trust you will enjoy reading this book. I also trust you will be challenged and choose to rise above every barrier of life that attempts to stop you from developing yourself and attaining your highest achievements.

STEP 1

DISCOVER

CHAPTER 1

THE JOURNEY OF DISCOVERY

The Noah Webster's 1828 dictionary defines "discover"
1. Literally, to uncover; to remove a covering
2. To lay open to the view; to disclose; to show; to make visible; to expose to view something before unseen or concealed. (*Job 12:22*)
3. To reveal; to make known (*Proverbs 25:2*)
4. To have the first sight of;
5. To find out; to obtain the first knowledge of; to come to the knowledge of something sought or before unknown.
6. To detect.

Discovery is the art of finding/learning something for the first time. It is a time when you find out you have the first knowledge about a thing. For example, the first time a lady finds out she is pregnant (If she had been expecting to get pregnant), she is ecstatic and overjoyed.

Discovering what your gift is brings a similar level of excitement. It fills you with a joy you cannot explain. You are not excited because the gift has manifested, you are excited because your mind begins to explore what you can do with the potential you have within you. It gives you a sense of expectancy because it makes you believe that with hard work, perseverance, and God's help, you can turn the gift into a success.

Discovering your Gift

A man's gift can do wonders! However, it can only do wonders if that man uses what he has. Some people do not even know that they have a gift hence it is of utmost necessity for a man to discover what his gift is or are. There are various methods to discover what your gifts are. We will be looking at 3 such ways:

1. By seeking God and asking him to show you what your gifts are.

Jeremiah 33:3 "Call to me, and I will answer you, and show you great and mighty things which you do not know"

Only a Manufacturer has all the details of making a product. If you need to know all the details of Samsung DVD player for example, you will have to read the manual that came with the DVD player or call the Samsung manufacturer.

The same is true with each individual. To find out the details of the gifts on the inside of us, we would need to seek our manufacturer (God). This time is when you set aside to spend quiet time in God's presence so he can speak to you about things you don't know and it's also a time when you talk to God. This time could be 10 minutes, 30 minutes or 1 hour. You decide what works for you.

> *Psalm 46:10a* (MSG) "Step out of the traffic! Take a long loving look at me, your High God,
> *Psalm 46:10a* (NLT) "Be still and know that I am God!"

There is something serene when you step out of traffic, there is something peaceful about solitude. Spending time with God can help make you less anxious about situations because when you choose to seek him about the situations in your life, you begin to see life from his perspective.

> *John 10:27* "My Sheep hear my voice and I know them and they follow me" (NKJV)

2a. Schedule time to Think and Imagine

Thinking time is also known as imagination time. Some of the definitions of the word, "Think" is "To have the mind engaged in reflection (to meditate)", "to have an expectation of (to anticipate), to reflect on(ponder), to center one's thoughts on (to form a mental picture of), to subject to the process of logical thoughts (to think things out).

The Bible says in *Proverbs 23:7a* "For as he thinks in his heart, so is he." (NKJV). The thoughts in a man's heart are what controls his life.

I should ask you a question. Are you able to imagine and think? I bet you are. The thoughts you have of yourself are what controls the direction of your life. Hence thinking time is when you spend time away alone, pondering, meditating and thinking things out. It is time when ideas come to light, it is time when you have the access to step into a world of imagination. What ideas do you have that you can use if you had no barriers? Imagination takes you to a world of unlimited possibilities. Ideas are products of thoughts. If you do not spend time to think, ideas cannot come. As ideas come, then you are able to imagine them and put them into action.

Imagination is the act or power of forming a mental image of something not present to the senses or never before wholly perceived in reality, it is the ability to think of new things, Imagination is creative ability. Imagination is so powerful, if only we know how powerful, we would tap into it.

According to Albert Einstein, "Your imagination is everything. It is a preview of life's coming attractions."

Napoleon Hill also said "Imagination is literally the workshop wherein are fashioned all plans created by man"

Why should we take time to imagine?

1. Imagination diminishes and eliminates the perception of obstacles. Imagination brings excitement when the two are combined, you will either not notice obstacles or they will be largely diminished and your courage will increase. David was not fazed by the height and strength of Goliath. He imagined victory and he got it.

2. You attract what you can imagine. When what you see in your imagination is bigger than what you see in reality, you will begin to attract the ideas, opportunities, resources, faith and relationship necessary to pursue those dreams.

3. Imagination stretches your mind to new possibilities. It stretches your mind and open it to new possibilities God wants to bring your way. "If you can see, you can have it." If you cannot imagine it, nothing will happen! What types of God-given possibilities can you imagine? You must begin to enlarge your ability to believe God for the impossible.

4. Imagination will help you to stop procrastinating. Imagination will get you out of "tomorrow" mentality about the things you feel God has placed in your heart. It awakens the dreams you buried for "someday." It eliminates fear and give your life direction and purpose.

5. Imagination will give your future a momentum. According to Mark Twain, "I can teach anybody how to get what they want in life. The problem is I can't

seem to find anybody who can tell me what they truly want." The future you imagine is the future you will arrive at. Imagination will give you the momentum to finish strong.

Ephesians 3:20a "Now to him who is able to do exceedingly abundantly above all that we ask or think"

What are you able to think, what are you able to imagine? In your thinking time, whatever God drops in your spirit, it is advisable to write it down and then God can give you further instructions and you will be astounded at what God will begin to open your eyes to, the ideas and the opportunities. You will really be amazed at what can result from "thinking time."

P. J. Daniels is a Christian businessman who had a disadvantaged background and was illiterate in his early years. However, after he met Christ in 1959, his life was changed around and he began to believe he was created to be somebody. He was a man that scheduled time to think. He reserved one day a week on his calendar just to think. He said all his ideas, opportunities and money making ventures started with the days he spent thinking.

Albert Einstein did his thinking in a special "thinking chair."

Successful people spend time alone. They use that time to think (of new innovations and ideas)

"Thinking precedes Achievement" *John Maxwell*

Successful people invest time to think about their future.

"Thinking is the hardest work there is, which is probably the reason only few people engage in it" *Henry Ford*

"The greater your thinking, the greater your achievements" *Terri Savelle Foy*

Thinking gives you direction to achieve what God will put your heart to do.

We sometimes believe we are too busy to engage in an activity. It is however necessary to first of all evaluate what the activity should be and if it should be done at all. We have to learn to take time to just sit there and spend time thinking.

"Some people say do something, I say "don't just do something, sit there and think" *Terri Savelle Foy*

If you don't just sit there to hear his voice, how do you follow his instructions? God wants to reveal your gifts to you and most of the time you will have to move away from the busyness of people and of things going on around you. You have to choose to sometimes spend time in isolation to reflect and think. You have two ears and one mouth for a reason. It's so that you can hear twice as much as you speak.

Thinking time is not talking time, it is imagination time, listening time. You however have to have a pen and a journal or and your electronic device ready to take notes as you receive instructions.

Thinking time is a time to imagine and meditate on your life in the future. The Bible says in *Ephesians 3:20* {AMP}

> "Now to Him who is able to [carry out His purpose and] do superabundantly more than all that we dare ask or think [infinitely beyond our greatest prayers, hopes, or dreams], according to His power that is at work within us"

Thinking time is the time to explore the possibilities in your mind.

As you practice being quiet before God, he will begin to reveal what he has created you for, what potentials you have and what gifts with which he has blessed you.

Habakkuk 2:1-2 (Message Translation)
What's God going to say to my questions? I'm braced for the worst.
I'll climb to the lookout tower and scan the horizon.
I'll wait to see what God says,
how he'll answer my complaint.
2-3 And then God answered: "Write this.
Write what you see.
Write it out in big block letters

2b. Have a Dream book/Dream board?
I do always take it a step further, it is something that I learnt from Terri Savelle Foy and it has really changed how I see my gifts and its manifestation. It's the idea of having a dream book and a dream board.

In your thinking corner, you should have a book you call a dream book, this is where you record all the ideas that come to you in your thinking time, I would also encourage you to have a dream board. A dream board is simply a cork board on which you put visual pictures that represent the visions, ideas and dreams you are trusting God to do in your life. The reason why it is important to have a dream board is because "What you see is what you become"

Do you have excellent culinary skills and plan on having a school where you could teach these skills and also having franchises all over your city in 5-10 years, why not get pictures of someone that has done a similar thing and put them on your dream board. A dream board makes ideas and dreams come alive, every time you see them.

It is not only good enough to have these on your dream board, put it where you can see it every day and schedule a time to pray over those dreams. It could be once a week, it could every night, it should be whatever what works for you. Those dreams might seem impossible but with hard work, diligence and God on your side, they will come to pass if you believe it. No matter how long they take, keep trusting God and keep working towards them until you see them come to pass.

3. Ask Questions

You need to ask yourself and ask other people questions to find out what your gifts are (your abilities, skills and talents).

The questions you ask are to be a guide, a starting point to find out what your gifts may be. You may wonder "Why questions"? The purpose of a question is to make you explore, a question makes you search, a question makes you dig deeper than what is on the surface.

Proverbs 25:2
"It is God's privilege to conceal things and the king's privileges to discover them." (NLT)

Everything that God has put on the inside of you is in hidden form and until you choose to make that discovery, you may never find out what gems and treasures you have on the inside of you. It is God's responsibility to hide those abilities in you and it is your responsibility to discover those abilities. Have you discovered all the treasures you have? It might be time for you to begin to do that today.

As you begin to ask questions, it would lead you on a journey of discovery. Such questions could be:
1. What do I love to do/what do I excited about doing?
2. What skills/talents do I have?
3. What am I good at/ best at doing?
4. What skills do I have that I can develop to impact my world?
5. What problems was I created to solve in this world?

6. What issues grieve me when I see or hear about them?
7. Am I creative person?
8. Am I a person that loves to work with my hands?
9. Do I love to make people laugh?
10. Do I have a strong attention to detail?
11. Am I a good communicator?
12. What can I do that I cannot fail at?
13. What ability do I have that no one else has like me?
14. What would other people say I am good at? (Ask three people)
15. Where do I like to spend time?
16. What do I like to make with my hands?
17. When I have free time, how do I spend It?
18. How do I like to help others?
19. What are my hobbies?
20. Am I arty in nature?
21. Do I love numbers?
22. Do I like the outdoors?
23. Do I like to build?
24. Do I love to organize things?
25. What do you think I am good at?

These are some of the questions you can ask yourself or ask others. I am sure you will come up with so many others. Asking questions causes you to pause and think, it also enables you to slow down and evaluate your life to see in what direction your life is going.

You might wonder what is the big deal about a gift. What if I don't have anything? No way! Everybody has "something", at least one that God has given you the ability to do. You just have to search and give yourself time to think.

CHAPTER 2

GIFTS ARE LIKE DREAMS

Gifts are truly like dreams, when you were a child you must have had a lot of dreams, "when I grow up, this is what I'm going to become". There were no limits, no barriers, nothing to stop it. However, as you became older, what happened? You and I stop dreaming. I remember when I was a little girl, I used to write short stories, make them up and keep them in my closet. I told myself when I grew up I was going to get all the stories published. I remember I had such an imagination and I could just go on and on writing for a long time but what guess happened when I grew up? I completely forgot about it. I let the day-to-day activities get ahead. I got busy with the mundane things of life and let my dream, my gift, slip away gradually. I got into the same routine that a lot of people get into today.

I neglected my gift, I refused to use my gift, I

failed to, I was careless about the gift God had endowed me with, that he has blessed me with.

That's my story. How about you? What has God blessed you with? What has he enabled used to do? What abilities and gifts have been given to you and what are you going to do with them.

Some people have the gift of singing but you never will hear them sing. Some have the gift of encouragement but you would never hear them talk. Some can cook the best meal ever but where are they? Some are the best artists but we would never know because they have put away their brushes to attend to a job while their gift wastes away. They don't want to challenge themselves with what God has endowed them with.

Proverbs 18:16
"A man's gift makes room for him. And bring him before great men." (NKJV)

"A gift does wonders; it will bring you before men of importance." The Living Bible

"Taking gifts to important people will help get you in to see them." New Century version

Giving a gift can open doors; it gives access to important people." New Living Translation

CHAPTER 3

YOUR DOMINANT GIFT

"A gift gets attention; It buys the attention of eminent people." The Message Bible.

The word "dominant" according to Cambridge Dictionaries means "more important", strong, or noticeable than anything else of the same type.

According to Oxford dictionaries, the word "dominant" means
1. having power and influence over others;(of a high place) overlooking others.

Noah Webster's dictionary describes dominant as
1. Ruling; prevailing, governing, predominant.

We can see that the word "dominant" means to subdue all others, to have power and influence over others. It means to be prevailing, governing, "the one in charge," ruling, predominant over others.

Each human being has gifts, skills, talents and abilities in him/her. However some of the gifts that you have in you will be more dominant than others.

Using myself as an example, I would say there are a couple of gifts that I believe I have. Some of such gifts are cooking, teaching, encouraging others, talking (now known as public speaking), writing singing and giving to others. however, I would say that the gifts I think has been most dominant in my life through the years will be that of teaching, writing and encouraging, inspiring and challenging others to be all that God has called them to be. I get most passionate when I am encouraging people to use their dominant gifts. It feels so natural.

Like I mentioned earlier, I started writing short stories when I was in elementary school. I had a good imagination and used to write different fictional stories which I told myself at the time that I was going to publish when I grew up. This however never happened because when I grew up, I got busy and moved on to do "more important" things. I did not even really do any writing until recently when I began to seek God regarding what he wanted me to do in my current season of life. He began to remind me how I used to write as a child and this brought back memories and a fresh challenge and love for writing.

Sometimes however there some of your dominant gifts that may lie dormant for years or even decades because you don't see it as a gift.

(The word "dormant" means "not in use.")

A lot of times, God has to use other people to challenge you in order for you to see that your gift is useful. For me, the gift that I did not see as useful was "talking." Growing up, I was known always known in as "the friend to all." I found it so easy to talk to people, I however did not see it as a gift. I used to think I talked too much and always tried to stop talking to people whenever I was in a new environment. It however did not work. My perspective however changed when I started watching Joyce Meyer on TV some years ago. I saw how her gift of talking was one of the gifts that God used to make her a blessing to her world. It made me realize that whatever we have the ability to do naturally, is not put in us by mistake. It is put in us so that we can be a blessing to our world.

For other people, your dominant gift could be acting, singing, making people laugh (being a comedian), playing an instrument and such like. It might even be an ability you have that seems weird, it could be an out-of-the box ability, it doesn't matter that people do not understand what it is.

I just told you a little bit about my story. What about you? What gift would you consider as your most dominant gift? Some people have one dominant gift.

Other people could have two or three. I found out that often a person will have two or three dominant gifts that work well together.

Examples of this could be Leadership and

Speaking, Writing and Speaking, Singing and Writing Songs, Playing Instruments and Singing, Event Planning and Catering, Interior Decorating and Designing, etc.

Irrespective of whether you have one dominant gift, two or three, the key is for you to discover that gift and harness it until it reaches its highest peak.

Action Time!

We have discussed a few ideas in this part of the book and I would love to challenge you to take some time to sit and ponder on the questions below. It might lead you on an adventure you have been waiting for...

Questions to ponder!

1. Have I made any discoveries?
2. What gifts do I have?
3. What needs do I love to meet in my sphere of influence?
4. What kind of problems attract my attention?
5. What am I passionate about?

STEP 2

DEVELOP

NOTES

CHAPTER 4

DEVELOPMENT IS A PROCESS

The word "develop" is defined as to design, create or improve an object or idea. It means to train, evolve or progress an individual or idea for a more focused reason.

"To develop" according to Noah Webster's 1828 dictionary means "to uncover, to lay open, to disclose or make known something concealed or withheld from notice. It means to unravel, to unfold what is intricate."

Development of your gift cannot however, be done solely by yourself. You will need a handful of people to come alongside to help you along the way to ensure this gift grows and advances to a of point excellence. Such people are mentors, teacher, trainers and coaches Your gift will most likely pass through various stages before it blossoms to the best it should be. I see development of your gift as an ongoing process.

The stage of preparation is where development starts however once training is initiated, birthing and nurturing are also essential in a gift coming into prominence hence a gift will inevitably go through a continuous form of training for it to be the best it should be.

Preparation

According to the business dictionary, "Preparation" is the state of making something ready for use. Preparations are typically done in anticipation of an event occurring in the near future.

Between the time of conception and delivery of a baby there is a time of preparation. It is a time when the new parents have to get ready for the birth of their child. God uses those nine months to prepare the parents' minds, he uses this period to expand their capacity in preparation for an addition to their lives. If a woman gets pregnant and had to give birth to the baby in 2 weeks or 4 weeks, I can imagine how unprepared that woman will be especially for a first time mother. Why does it have to take as long as nine months? I believe that as the baby grows in a woman's tummy, the more the woman's capacity grows to take care of that baby when he or she arrives. It is a period when she grows physically, psychologically (in relation to the baby), mentally, develops a love for the little creature growing in her, feeds the baby and develops a bond with that child.

The same way a baby grows, a person with a gift needs that period of developing that gift and making it ready to manifest. This period of preparation is a period when your gift is put through rigorous training to bring forth the best from it. Remember one of the definitions of "develop" means to" train." "Training" here means the act or process of drawing or educating; education. Let's seek to look at the various forms of training a person's gift will need.

NOTES

CHAPTER 5

DEVELOPMENT THROUGH TRAINING

Forms of training

1.Training your ears to hear instructions from God.

God is our creator and he alone is the one who reveals to us the gift he has placed in us and hence to effectively deploy that gift, it is imperative for us to consistently go back to him to direct us, lead us and instruct us regarding using that gift.

The more you sit at his feet, the more you are tuned to him. It allows you to know his voice and hear his leading even in the midst of noise.

Proverbs 4 1-2 (NKJV)
"Hear, my children the instruction of a father, and give attention to know understanding".

Proverbs 2:1-8 (NKJV)

My son, if you receive my words, And treasure my commands within you, [2] So that you incline your ear to wisdom, And apply your heart to understanding; [3] Yes, if you cry out for discernment, And lift up your voice for understanding, [4] If you seek her as silver, And search for her as for hidden treasures; [5] Then you will understand the fear of the Lord, And find the knowledge of God. [6] For the Lord gives wisdom; From His mouth come knowledge and understanding; [7] He stores up sound wisdom for the upright; He is a shield to those who walk uprightly; [8] He guards the paths of justice, And preserves the way of His saints.
New King James Version (NKJV)

As we sit at his feet, he guides us, gives us wisdom, understanding, knowledge, discernment, and preserve our ways. He makes sure we don't make mistakes, he reveals secrets to us, he teaches us in ways others may not have access to and he opens our eyes to opportunities to use that gift. (Proverbs 4:10 -21) It is so essential to train our ears to hear him and our heart to receive those instructions, it will take us places.

2. Training your ears to hear instructions given by Mentors/Coaches

Who are Mentors and Coaches? Those two words seem similar but are different.

Coaching is:

"...a process that enables learning and development to occur and thus performance to improve. To be successful, a Coach requires a knowledge and understanding of process as well as the variety of styles, skills and techniques that are appropriate to the context in which the coaching takes place" Eric Parsloe, The Manager as Coach and Mentor (1999) page 8. Eric is a respected author and Director of the OCM

Mentoring is:

"...off-line help by one person to another in making significant transitions in knowledge, work or thinking." Clutterbuck, D & Megginson, D, Mentoring Executives and Directors (1999) page 3. David Clutterbuck & David Megginson are both founder members of The European Mentoring and Coaching Council and highly respected authors, academics and consultants in the mentoring arena.

Mentors and Coaches are people who come alongside a person to help them recognize and accomplish all they need to do. They are people who have the capability to help a person reach their next level. They also have the ability to draw out the best in a person by challenging those people.

Mentors resolves more around developing the mentee professionally while coaching resolves more around specific development areas or issues. Coaching and mentoring use the same skills and approach but coaching is short term task-based and mentoring is a longer term relationship.

The differences between a Coach and a Mentor?

Mentoring
- Ongoing relationship that can last for a long period of time
- Can be more informal and meetings can take place as and when the mentee needs some advice, guidance or support
- More long-term and takes a broader view of the person
- Mentor is usually more experienced and qualified than the 'mentee.' Often a senior person in the organization who can pass on knowledge, experience and open doors to otherwise out-of-reach opportunities
- Focus is on career and personal development
- Agenda is set by the mentee, with the mentor providing support and guidance to prepare them for future roles
- Mentoring resolves more around developing the mentee professional

Coaching
- Relationship generally has a set duration
- Generally, more structured in nature and meetings are scheduled on a regular basis
- Short-term (sometimes time-bounded) and focused on specific development areas/issues
- Focus is on development/issues at work
- Coaching is generally not performed on the

basis that the coach needs to have direct experience of their client's formal occupational role, unless the coaching is specific and skills-focused

- The agenda is focused on achieving specific, immediate goals
- Coaching revolves more around specific development areas/issues

The reason why I am taking time to define these terms is so that you can know the difference and use those differences to determine which one is appropriate for you to have. Another thing you have to know is that even though you have either a coach or mentor., It is your responsibility to follow training routines and instructions as your mentors instruct you, you have a responsibility to follow your routine strictly on the instructions of the mentors.

As an athlete, you do not allow your body to dictate to you. Rather you dictate to your body what it should do. You put it through hard training as is deemed necessary. Some athletes wake up as early as 3 a.m. to train and even though it may not be convenient, it may be necessary to attain the goal-ahead. Whatever skill, talent, gift or ability you are set to develop, following a trainer's (coaches', mentors') instructions is key to attaining the highest level of progress possible. It will also go a long way to determine whether your gift is improved in quality and whether your gift will attain the required level of excellence.

The Importance of a Mentor/Coach in a person's life.

If you have a gift of any sort, seeking out leaders to help you develop yourself is key. It is so important to seek out mentors, people who have successfully excelled in your field. If you are called to a marriage ministry, outreach ministry or any other similar one, seek out mentors in these fields, if you are called to make impact in your community, seek out people that have done this successfully and begin to study them. This can be done from afar or by meeting with them on a regular basis depending on your geographical location and theirs. (That is where books, CDs, DVDs, MP3s come in)

Whatever gift you need to deploy to your world, learn to stand on the shoulders of others. Seek to learn from your mentors, coaches and trainers. It will make your journey easier and you will learn from their mistakes.

- Mark Zukerberg had Steve Jobs as his mentor
- Sir Richard Branson had Sir Freddie Laker as his mentor
- Dr Martin Luther king Jr. had a mentor Dr. Benjamin May
- Joshua's mentor was Moses
- Napoleon Hill's mentor was Andrew Carnegie
- Paul learnt from Gamaliel
- Paul was Timothy's mentor

- Fashion designer Christian Dior mentored designer Yves St. Laurent
- Bill Clinton had a mentor, J.William Fulbright
- Oprah Winfrey had a mentor, Maya Angelou
- Ronaldo (a soccer player) learnt from Laszlo Bodoni, his coach
- Barack Obama learnt from Frank Marshall Davis, his mentor.
- Stephen Curry had a coach, Bob Mckillop
- Kenneth Copeland had mentors, Kenneth E. Hagin & Oral Roberts
- Pastor Enoch Adeboye had a mentor, Pa. Akindayomi.
- Bill Gates had a mentor, Warren Buffett

Who is your mentor, coach, trainer or teacher?

Below is an excerpt of Usain Bolt's statement of his coach Glen Mills.

"Usain has been coached by Glen Mills since 2004 and he has been a major factor in turning the talented junior into the World's Fastest Man. Usain describes Coach Mills as a father figure and someone who guides him both on and off the track, "He has always made the right decisions for me. He is a guiding light in my career and he has shown me the way to improve myself both as a person and as an athlete," said Bolt after his 2008 Olympic success.
Coach Mills has worked with some of the

Caribbean's top sprinters since the 1970's with athletes such as two-time Olympic finalist Raymond Stewart, 2003 100m World Champion Kim Collins and 2004 Olympic relay gold medalist Aileen Bailey.

He is the head of Racers Track Club which currently produces many of Jamaica's top athletes including 2011 World 100m Champion Yohan Blake and 400m stars Rosemarie Whyte and Jermaine Gonzales.

Coach Mills has been the head coach on many Jamaican teams at Olympic Games and World Championships. He first started coaching at his alma mater, Camper Down High in East Kingston, and developed it into a sprinting powerhouse nick-named 'Sprint Factory'.

He has earned diplomas from the International Olympic Committee training centre in Mexico and High-Level Sprint Tech training at the IAAF Training Centre in Puerto Rico. Mills was honored in 2008 by receiving the IAAF Coach of the Year award as well as been named NACAC Coach of the Year during the 18th Congress of the NACAC Track and Field Coaches Association.

3. Training your mind by educating yourself formally or informally

(This could be in form of attending classes, seminars, conferences or maybe having to go to college.)

The type of gift you have is what will determine the kind of education and training you will require. Some gifts may require some form of formal education and others may not. Whatever you require, you still have to carry out your research to find out how to enhance your gift and take it to the highest level of prominence. Some people may be required to go back to college, some may be required to go to a trade school, some may need to just attend seminars or sign up for a coaching and mentoring program, some may need to take online classes, some however may just need to find a mentor to show them the path to take. It is necessary to do an extensive research on how to harness one's gift.

Whatever your gift requires, it is time to take it to the next level. Do you need to apply for a particular course in the next school year, why not start the application today? do not wait till the last minute. Do you just need to do a short course at the Continuing Education Center? Go for it. Time does not wait for anyone. It keeps ticking so don't waste any more time. If all your gift needs are a mentor or coach, it's time to seek one out and begin to learn from them.

4. Training your character to work in harmony with your gifts.
You might wonder why it is important for your gifts to work in harmony with your character?

Over the decades, statistics have shown that if you don't have the right character, it may deter the longevity of your gifts. According to the Merriam-Webster Dictionary, a person's character is the way someone thinks feels and behaves. It describes a person's personality. Your character is your way of thinking, your attitudes, it is the features or traits that form an individual's nature. It is one's reputation, the mental and moral qualities distinctive to an individual. it is your personality, nature, disposition, temperance, temper, mentality, makeup, it is your identity. it is your moral or ethical quality that helps you to choose either wrong or right at every point in time. When your character is adequately trained, it will gradually impact on how your gift will be demanded or if it will be demanded.

I will like us to look at some examples of people who did not train their gift to work in harmony with their character. Training here indicates controlling your character positively.

4.1. Royston Drenthe

It is all too easy to forget just how highly rated Royston Drenthe was at one time. Having already become a Feyenoord regular, he made a huge impression at the 2007 U-21 European championships in which the Netherlands won the tournament and Drenthe was named best player. He immediately became one of the hottest prospects in Europe, joining Real Madrid for about $20 million dollars that summer. Drenthe fell out with the management at both Hercules and Everton even admitting "My attitude and poor mentality ruined my career there" He now plays in the Arabian Gulf League.

4.2. Adriano

Famed for his incredible shot power and almost comical inconsistency. Adriano had all the tools to become a world-class forward but instead used them to become a world-class fool. Luis Figo best summed it up when he said "Adriano is a classic example of how to destroy your talent" adding "Talent is secondary though, if you do not balance it with dedication and professionalism". Two things he completely lacked. Adriano's poor attitude allowed him to be unfit and in the last 4 years prior to the end of his career, he played less than 20 matches. By the time he was 33, he was without a club.

4.3. O.J. Simpson

O.J. Simpson was born in 1947 in San Francisco, California. He became a college football star at USC, winning the Heisman Trophy in 1968, and later enjoyed a record-setting career in the NFL. Amid a moderately successful post-playing career as an actor and broadcaster, Simpson was charged in 1994 for murdering his former wife, Nicole Brown Simpson, and her friend Ron Goldman. He was acquitted in a high-profile criminal trial, though he was found liable for their deaths in civil court. Simpson later was sentenced to up to 33 years in prison in 2008 for kidnapping and armed robbery.

4.4. Mike Tyson

Born in Brooklyn, New York, on June 30, 1966, Mike Tyson became the youngest heavyweight boxing champion of the world in 1986, at age 20. He lost the title in 1990 and later served three years in prison over rape charges. He subsequently earned further notoriety by biting Evander Holyfield's ear during a rematch in 1997. Tyson has gone on to appear in several films, including a documentary and Broadway show on his life.

5. Training your body: this will be essentially if you have a talent or a skill that is highly technical such as is required in a sport.

Usain Bolt is an athlete who knows the value of training and in a recent interview explained why training is essential to getting better in sports.

Interviewer: How do you train for Speed? Any specific tips for training to become faster

UB: There are many things the help someone run faster, conditioning, strength, speed, power technique, and such like. It is not just one factor. You have to train in a variety of ways and cover all the aspects

Interviewer: What is a typical training session ?

UB: there isn't really a typical session. Training

for me is either on the track or in the gym. It depends on the time of year and what we are working on. On the track it can be working on everything from endearing to any technical aspect of my race., the transition for both the hundred meter and 200 meters. In the gym it's General conditioning, strength and power.

Interviewer: How how often do you train?

UB: I train 4-11 months of the year, six days a week. Normally in the morning and then again in the afternoon it's a lot of work.

Interviewer: What does training do for you other than the physical benefits?

UB: Training gives you confidence and this helps your state of mind. I know if I'm in good shape it's going to be very hard to beat me.

Interviewer: What kind of obstacles have you faced and overcome to achieve your goals?

UB: Elite Sports Injury is always the same that can slow you down as we push our bodies to the Max and sometimes we get sore injured muscles or joints. I had several injuries in my career but fortunately I have a good coach and team to help me get back to the top.

Interviewer: Any particular food and drinks that help you when your training? Are you still liking chicken nuggets?

UB: I have a good diet now and I have a chef who helps me. A lot of chicken, rice, vegetable. Good Jamaican food. It is also important to be well hydrated.

Interviewer: What is your advice for someone struggling to find motivation to reach the goal?

UB: You have to find that one thing that you know is going to motivate you. You might not enjoy training for example but you have to love competing and winning if you want these things you have to be determined and train heart to yours house training changed a lot for you in the past year movie when I started running as a kid it was fun. I was good at it so I just did it. I didn't really have to train that much to win races, as I got older I realized that I have to take better care of my body. Now diet, rest, recovery is more important than a few years ago.

Interviewer: What's your single greatest goal?

UB: My single greatest goal is to become the greatest, pretty much. That's what I work for. I want to be remembered as a great Sportsman, to have a place in history.

Interviewer: What other Athlete inspires you to become better?

UB: You know I have always admired Kevin Garnett as he is a player that whether winning or losing he gives his all and inspires those around him to raise their game. Also my mentor and coach Glen Mills. He used to tell me: "Everybody on the circuit, everybody at the Championships are talented athletes already. It's the work you put in that makes you a champion, or better that the other talented person."

Action Time!

While reading the development step of this book, there may have been some ideas that came to your mind while reading, you might have realized there are some steps you need to take, here is your time to do this. I have listed some questions below to aid you in taking action. These questions are however just a guide, please feel free to add to them.

Questions to ponder

1. Are there any God-given instructions that I have ignored?
2. Does my gift need any form of training?
3. What action plans do I need to put in place?
4. Where do I go from here?

NOTES

STEP 3

DEPLOY

NOTES

CHAPTER 6

WHAT DOES IT MEAN TO DEPLOY YOURSELF?

Deployment has to do with the use of your gift. In this part of the book, we will be exploring what it means to birth, nurture your gift while it's in use. We will also look at the obstacles that try to stop you from using it and the harnessing of your potentials.

The word Deployment means "the use of something or someone in a reflective way."

To be deployed means to be used in the best way possible. Deployment is the place where your gift comes alive. It is the place of use. After the time of preparation for a baby, the birth is waited upon. When you have trained your gift, it is time to manifest, it's time to show up.

Deploying involves action. You might wonder how do I deploy myself? The secret is to start from where you are. You might be thinking of starting a catering business, interior decoration business, delivery services, no matter what it is; start small, look at your neighbourhood and see how you can meet a need there. You can use social media to promote yourself. You must also seek to be the best because if you are excellent, you will grow and attract those that need your service.

Let's explore what deploying yourself entails. Once the period of preparation is over, the gift is ready to come to a stage of manifestation. The gift manifesting is when the gift really begins its journey. At this stage, all the training from the mentors, coaches, teachers and training from formal or informal education will be put to use.

Start from where you are!

The Place of Birthing and Nurturing

Birthing time is not time to hide, No! It is time to begin to walk in the ability of that gift. For example, you might have a gift in making people's hair beautiful. To really deploy that gift professionally, most of the time you would have gone to a college to further enhance the use of that gift. Birthing time is the time to let that gift shine, it is the time to put in all your efforts to ensure that gift is known.

Birthing time is the time to access every opportunity God is bringing your way. These could range from job opportunities, opportunities at events or hair shows, opportunities with your family members whereby you could give them haircuts and hair-do's to showcase what you are about.

The advantage of doing this is that it shows what kind of gift you have and how good you are. It could also open up other opportunities for you.

Why Nurturing?

You may wonder, why do you need to nurture a gift, it is already in use, isn't that good enough? Nurturing is essential to a gift. It is as essential as continuous care is necessary to a child.

According to the Cambridge Dictionary, to 'nurture' means to take care of, feed and protect someone or something especially young children and help them develop. To nurture also means to help a plan or a person to develop and be successful.

According to dictionary.com, Nurturing is the process of caring for and encouraging the growth or development of someone or something. It denotes you nourishing the gifts of God in you. At this point you might want to stop and ponder over the following statements.

Are you nourishing the gifts you have or are they diminishing in your life?

Are they growing?

Are they getting better or dying slowly?

You alone have the answers to these questions.

Nurturing your gift is the care and attention you give to the gift while it is in use. Nurturing also involves making sure your gift is protected while it's in use. Nurturing is the polishing of a gift. It is the care that you give to it.

NOTES

CHAPTER 7

STIR IT UP: NO MORE BARRIERS

What does it mean to "stir a thing up?" To stir up a thing means to keep using that thing, to affect strongly, to incite; to move briskly, to move from inactivity.

To stir up here means in the environment where you are, affect it strongly, use what he has put inside of you, the gift he has given you for your generation.

It means to "incite" – to incite means to move into action. Stop sitting on your oars, stop waiting on people to help you. Decide to start (Stop "trying" to start) just do it. Remember, the world is waiting for you and me to manifest, when are we going to manifest? When are you going to be revealed, when am I going to be revealed?

How do I stir up my gift?

Paul spoke to Timothy in *2nd Timothy 1:6* about "stirring up his gift."

"Therefore I remind you to stir up the gift of God which is in you through the laying on of my hands" – *2ⁿᵈ Tim.1:6* (NKJV)

Paul was Timothy's mentor hence he wanted to see timothy become all that he could be. Paraphrased, Paul was saying to him "All I have taught you, all that you have caught, don't let it go to waste. Don't let it lie dormant, use it."

"Stir it up" means "Use it." "Affect your environment." "Stand out." Paul was saying to Timothy here, "I have done my part, I have laid hands on you. Now you have to do your part which is to develop your gift and use it." Paul could not do that part for Timothy.

In the same way, God has deposited a gift or multiple gifts in you. You however have the responsibility of deciding whether you will let it lie dormant in you or whether you will develop it and use it. God will not come down and use it for you.

"I heard the story of a lady, while listening to one of Bill Winston's audio messages (paraphrased)

There was a certain pastor in Costa Rica who just got fed up with the way things were going in the country economically that he decided to do something about it.

He came to church one day and started giving people small amounts of money. As he gave it to them, he would say, "Use your gift and this money to bring about some change in your sphere of influence." As he came to this lady, he gave her about $15 or $20. She however refused to take it saying that her husband had just left her and she had 3 children and did not know how to do anything. The pastor persisted explaining that there must be something that she knew how to do. Eventually she took it saying, she only knew how to make pancakes for her children. He said to her "start from there, make pancakes and take them to the market and sell them to workers."

The very next morning, she made pancakes and took them to the market place and they sold out. She was so excited that she came and told the pastor. He told her to make more and take them the next day. The next day she did the same thing and they sold out again. Gradually, word began to spread about her pancakes and she got better at making them. Soon her business got bigger and after a while, she opened up a catering business, began to expand and soon people began to come from all over the city and provinces to learn how she was doing so well. Her business began to boost the economy of the city in which she lived and soon word got to the president of the country who called her to see how her business sense could be reproduced all over the country.

This lady did not know she had this gift as it was lying dormant, until the pastor challenged her. She decided to give it a try, since she had nothing to lose. Once she got stirred up, and chose to use her gift, God began to bring her into prominence. You can do the same today.

No more Barriers

Look at the story of the man at the pool of Bethesda in John 5:1-11. He had been there for thirty-eight years and things did not change because he refused to make an effort. Instead he made excuses. He could at least try maybe to roll towards the water, tumble, ask for help or at least do something. He didn't, he just laid there, waiting.

Thirty-eight years is a long time to be at one spot but he did not seem to see that. Jesus asked him one question and he started to ramble off excuses.

Vs. 5b- "Do you want to be made well?" He answered with an excuse.

Vs.7 – "The sick man answered him "Sir, I have no man to put me into the pool when the water is stirred up; but while I am coming, another steps down before me."

Can you imagine, for thirty-eight years, he could not figure out a way to get to the pool before any other man. It was not yet so important to him to be without his infirmity. He let that infirmity become a barrier to everything he was to be in life. He let that infirmity dictate his whole life. He refused to take responsibility for his own life. He left his life to the mercy of other men. "I have no one to put me in."

Jesus only gave him 3 instructions.

1. Rise
2. Take up your bed
3. Walk

Jesus indicated the man should not let others define him. He should not let them determine how far he could go. He had to make a choice to go forward and do whatever he had to do to advance in life.

Be ready to rise above all the circumstances of life. We all have messes that we have been through but our messes are meant to become a message. It's not meant to be buried, It's meant to encourage someone else going through the same situation or a similar situation. Our messes are what shows our God off when they become a message we use. Only that man could decide to rise, Jesus could not decide for him.

He had to take up his bed, referring to challenging himself. Taking up his bed was not easy because he had not done it in thirty-eight years but it was time for action. No more excuses were to be allowed in his life. He had to walk, everywhere he went now, his life was speaking because his testimony was obvious, he could walk. He was no longer lame, he could make choices he had not made in a long time.

Being lame could refer to various situations in our lives. Whatever has held you stagnant, held you bound, hindered you from moving forward and advancing to your destined place in life is your lame position.

What is that barrier that you are letting hold you back, what is the obstacle stopping your gift from manifesting? A lot of people do not use their gifts because they see obstacles.

I once saw a quote that said "Obstacles are stepping stones to your success".

When you learn to see obstacles as stepping stones and not road blocks, they will aid you in your journey of life. Such obstacles could be:

- lack of funds (what would you do if you had unlimited funds?)
- past life experiences
- low self esteem
- fear of being laughed at
- fear of failure
- fear of "I have nothing to give"
- just fear, fear of people not buying into your vision
- belonging to a minority race
- lack of confidence
- political obstacles
- yourself (That's the biggest excuse or barrier that can stop a person)
- other excuses not mentioned here

I found some quotes on excuses that I found pretty interesting.

1. "At the end of the day, let there be no excuses, no explanations, no regrets." *Dr Steve Maraboli*

2. Quit Making excuses
   Putting it off
   Complaining about it
   Dreaming about it

Whining about it
Crying about it
Believing you can't
Worrying if you can't
Waiting. Suck it up
Hold on Tight. Say a prayer
Make a Plan and Just
DO IT
Make your own at Electricfairground.com

3   Excuses will always be there for you; Opportunity won't.
Fitnessquotes.net

4. There are only two options: Make progress or make excuses. *Unknown*

5.   Success occurs when your dreams get bigger than your excuses. *Unknown*

So quit making excuses today. Get up and walk, if you can't walk, crawl, if you can't crawl, sit down, if you can't sit down, lie down, if you can't lie down just do something.

In an attempt to deploy your gift, the road may not be smooth, you however have to decide to overcome every challenge and get to the finish line. Challenges are distractions, they seek to take your eyes off the goal if you let them.

When athletes are running a marathon for instance, people normally would stand on the sides cheering them on. Do they stop and say hello to those people? No. Even when they are offered water to quench their thirsts, they don't stop, they drink as they run. It is a marathon, a race. They cannot afford to stop and chat, rest or observe what is going on around them either. No. Deployment time is time to work. They have trained so hard just to get here.

The same way when you have trained your gift through mentors, coaches, education and your character has been trained, now is the time to shine. Now is the time to use your gift.

I could go on and on but the Bible says in *1ˢᵗ John 4:4b*(NKJV)

"He who is you is greater than he who is in the world"

When God is with us, we have no fear, he will help us but we have to let every obstacle we come across become a stepping stone in using our gift. Do not despair, be confident in God, he has equipped you, go forth and walk in his might.

CHAPTER 8

YOUR POTENTIAL MUST NOT BE WASTED

We have been referring to the gifts you have on the inside of you.

May I ask you some questions?

Is your gift being a blessing to anyone?

Does anybody even know that you have a gift?

Has anybody benefited from the potentials you have?

"Potential" is defined as "something existing in possibility but not in act." It is defined as "anything that may be possible" but that's only if you let it. That is sad isn't it? To have all the potential that the Almighty has placed on the inside of you but it is not being used. When you don't use it, it is wasted. How sad!

Can you imagine when you get to heaven and God asks what you did with all the potential He put on the inside of you. What would you say?

Would you say "I could not find a way to use it so I set it aside."

Maybe God created you to be a scientist, to discover so many inventions to impact your world but because of obstacles, you decided "it's not worth it" so your potential ended up wasted.

Do you know from information gathered, it has been discovered that the richest place on earth is the cemetery? It is because a lot of people come to earth with potential. God put gifts, skills and talents in each of us but when we do not harness it, it remains as wasted potential lying dormant until we go to meet our maker. I pray this would not be your story or my story.

When Myles Munroe died, the world grieved, but one thing that was continually remembered about him was his mantra of dying empty. His greatest advocacy was for a human being to come to this world, be a blessing to his world and die empty. We can truly say Myles Munroe died empty because he was such a blessing to his world while he was here and through his books and messages.

Would that be your story when it's time to meet your maker. What would be said about you, if you had the opportunity to write about your life just a few minutes before you die?

Would you say you have lived a full life? Would you say you have given all you have in you? Would you say you have been a blessing to your generation and generations after you? What would be your story?

Some people have books on the inside of them, some have songs the world will never hear, some have leadership qualities that the world will never see because they have decided to do nothing with what has been given to them. Gifts can be developed, they can be harnessed, they can be taken to a new level only if the person with the gift decides to do so.

Action Time

Has God given you ideas that would make the world go Wow... but nobody has heard about it? What are you waiting for? Remember there are some people God has decided you will impact, they are waiting.

Think about it today What are you doing with your potentials? Remember you will have to give an account to your maker.

Questions to ponder.

1. Are there some decisions you need to take today?
2. Are there some actions you need to put in place?
3. What is God asking you to do to enhance your journey to prominence?
4. What excuses have you been making in your life that you need to get rid of?
5. What have been your barriers/obstacles to greatness?

NOTES

STEP 4

A PLACE OF PROMINENCE

NOTES

CHAPTER 9

HOW DO I GET THERE?

A place of prominence according to Noah Webster's 1828 dictionary is a place of "shooting forward," a place of standing out from the surface of something.

According to Google online dictionary, the word "Prominent" means:

1. The state of being important or famous
2. The fact or condition of standing out from something by physically projecting or being particularly noticeable.

According to the free dictionary.com, Prominent means:

1. Projecting outward or upward from a line or surface
2. Immediately noticeable, conspicuous
3. Widely known; eminent

When a person seeks to get to a place of prominence, it is up to that person to develop what he has in his hands, in his heart (a mission) or in his house (referring to your talent, skill or gift) to its best ability and then bring it in contact with his "vessel or vessels."

The Woman with the jar of oil

A lot of times, we live ignorant of the gifts or tools God has placed in us or around us in our everyday lives. The woman in (*2ⁿᵈ Kings 4:1-7*) was ignorant of how important that jar of oil was. She almost lost her two sons because of her ignorance. You might be looking at her situation, what about yours, what is the jar of oil in your house? Could it be your voice, your listening abilities, your ability to make people laugh, your ability to create witty inventions, your ability to use numbers like nobody else... What is yours?

All that woman needed to do was to bring her jar of oil in contact with the vessels to start her journey to prominence. The place of prominence comes when your developed gifts collide with your "vessels."

Our vessels are:
1. the opportunities God has put around us,
2. problems we were created to solve,
3. leveraging – using other people's knowledge and ideas, plaforms, failures and successes.

1. The opportunities around us:

"There are opportunities that are passing us everyday and we are either seizing them or letting them go." *Oral Roberts*

An opportunity can be paraphrased as an "open door." It is however, only open for a certain time hence we hear people say "I missed that opportunity." There was a season in my life that I missed quite a few opportunities because I just did not access the 'open door' at the right time. This made me start making a certain declaration everyday "I am surrounded by opportunities and I am sensitive to the Holy Spirit to help me see them, my steps are ordered by God." I also began to make a conscious effort to notice what was going on around me more and trust God to alert me when an opportunity came along.

Here is a famous quote most people know:
"Opportunity + Preparation = Success."

It really is true. When your gift is prepared and it comes in contact with an opportunity, success is inevitable. A lot of people don't prepare for their moment. You never know when your opportunity will come so like the Boys Scouts motto, always "Be Prepared."

2. Problems we were created to solve:
There are some specific problems that you were created to solve. There were problems that I was created to solve and those problems have our names on it.

The way we know is that whenever we see these problems in our environment or elsewhere, we feel drawn to them. Another way we can tell is that you develop an interest in those problems whenever you hear of it.

For someone that has the gift of organization, that person hates it when anything is out of place. He/she feels like they have to put what is out of place in its rightful place. Exploring the opportunities in this field will take these kind of people to a higher level if they are just willing to put in the work and diligence needed to harness the gift they have.

For some people, they could sit and listen to a person talk for hours without interrupting and they could comprehend what he/she is saying at the same time. Such people have a gift of listening. As you take time to discover, remember discovery comes in the place of thinking, spending time with God and asking yourselves and others questions.

3. Leveraging:

3a. The first way you can leverage is by using other people's knowlege and ideas.
(reading their books and listening to their messages)

What exactly does the word "leverage" mean? Leverage simply means the use of influence or power to achieve a desired result. Depending on what your gift is, you can use other people's ideas (that you read in their books, listening to their audio CD's, watch online, watch on TV or any social media medium) to boost you to another level. The good thing about books is that if you are reading the book of a person that is doing what you want to do, maybe you have similar gifts, you would learn the mistakes he made hence you may be learning from 10, 20, 30 years of experience. This would save you going the long route, in his book, the person may suggest ways of doing it better which he found out after making several mistakes.

"The more
That you read,
The more things you will know
The more that you learn,
The more places you'll go"
Dr Seuss

3b. The second way you can leverage is by using other people's platforms.

This can be in the form of attending their training sessions, coaching classes or mentorship with them. Examples of these are John Maxwell's team, Brian Tracy's team, Jack Canfield's team, Michael Hyatt's team and other similar teams.

Earlier on, we spoke of Usain Bolt's coach, Glen Mills who helped Usain get to prominence. The training drills, schedules and disciplines his coach mapped out and his determination to deploy his gift to the highest level brought him and brought him to a place of prominence.

3c. The third way you can leverage is by using other people's failures.

"Leveraging means using something to carry a weight beyond your ability"-Matthew Ashimolowo. Leveraging using Other Peoples' failures teaches you how not to do things. Where people have failed, they teach us not to repeat their failures.

In learning from other peoples' failures, you have to ask questions why that person failed. When you do this, you are able to use their failure to rise and make progress, you are also able to use their failures to learn. You learn that even if you failed at a business, it does not make you a failure. The business might have failed but you are not a failure if you fail at a project, you have to choose to not stay down but to get up and keep going.

Proverbs 24:16-"For a righteous man may fall seven times and rise again but the wicked shall fall by calamity' -NKJV

3d. The fourth way you can leverage is by using other people's success.

Why would you need to do this? Because a person that has gone ahead of you and excelled in what you want to do gives you insight you might not have.

Learning from other people's success is like asking them questions about their success. It involves reading their books (if you do not have direct access to them), it involves you watching their lives and observing them closely to see how they do things and what disciplines they observe. It involves learning their secrets as this could act as a lever to propel you to greater increase.

Queen Sheba was a very prominent queen. She was a woman of great wealth, beauty and power according to the biblical scholars. Sheba, believed to be from either Ethopia or Yemen, was a well-established city and although there is little evidence outside the bible as to the nature of the monarchy and how it was established, it is clear that the Queen of Sheba ruled alone and was not enamoured with the religions in her own land.

Regardless of her prominence, she travelled to Jerusalem to see King Solomon when She heard of his fame to ask him questions and see if he was really as wise as She had heard he was. She came to observe what could make her kingdom even greater. She came to learn what could make her rise further than she already was. (1st Kings 10)

Success is never an accident. It is a progressive walk. There are laws that govern success and when you see a successful person, you should seek to know what has enhanced that person's success.

Successful people always pay a high price which you don't have to pay when learning from them. You can enjoy the benefits without paying the price they paid, without going through the suffering and pains, difficulties and disappointments they went through.

We must study successful people to become more successful.

NOTES

CHAPTER 10

DILIGENCE AND EXCELLENCE: YOU WILL STAND BEFORE GREAT MEN!

Do you aspire to be great? I'm sure you do. Guess what, Great men are not found at the bottom, they are found at the top.

"Great" means an extent, amount or intensity considerably above the normal or average.

To get to a place of prominence, it's time to leave the normal and the average. It's time to begin to aspire for the excellence and the greatness that is only found at the top.

Greatness here connotes all we have been discussing in this book. The need to develop your gift, the need for training and the need to be diligent with that gift.

Diligence

Let's consider what the word "diligent" connotes in *Proverbs 21:5*.

NKJV: "The plans of the diligent leads surely to plenty but those of everyone who is hasty, surely to poverty"

NLT: "Good Planning and hard work leads to prosperity, but hasty shortcuts lead to poverty"

The Message Bible: "Careful planning puts you ahead in the long run; hurry and scurry puts you further behind."

When you hear that word "diligence," what comes to mind is normally hard work. I checked out the meaning of diligence in the dictionary, it means

"the steady application in business of any kind; constant effort to accomplish what is undertaken; exertion of body or mind without unnecessary delay or sloth, giving something it's due attention."

I once heard:
"Diligence is the philosophers stone that turns everything to gold." *Unknown*

I think where a lot of us have a challenge is being "up today and down tomorrow". There is no consistency and that is the main difference between a diligent man and a slothful man.

Diligence, in Christianity, is the effort to do one's part, while keeping faith and reliance in God.

Diligence was one of the virtues that enabled Daniel to stand out in Babylon. In every assignment he was given by the king, he was diligent as such that his diligence and his excellence caused him to stand out in a strange land.

"What we hope to do with ease, must first be done with diligence." *Samuel Johnson*

"Everything yields to diligence." *Antiphanes*

"Patience and diligence, like faith, remove mountains." *William Penn*

"The 5 D's to Success; desire, direction, discipline, diligence, dedication." *Mark Munoz*

"Diligent hands will rule, but laziness ends in slave labor" *Proverbs 12:24*

Excellence

In this section, we want to examine what that word excellence means.

To excel means to go beyond, to exceed, to surpass in good qualities, to outdo.

It also means to perform actions to an unusual degree, to be eminent, illustrious or distinguished.

You can see excellence means to go above the normal, to surpass expectations.

When you do things the normal way, do you stand out? No! You don't usually because that is what everybody is doing but when you complete a task in an unusual manner or do you solve a problem no other person can solve, what happens? You are noticed because you went over and beyond"

God is calling us to a life of excellence. Whenever you find yourself in whatever career or vocation,

God would be known when you are excellent. Do you know why. Excellence attracts! Do you notice that. Everybody wants to identify with excellence. When a task is done excellently, everybody wants to know who did it.

At work, if you choose to become excellent at all you do, guess what? You will be noticed. As believers, you have an edge of knowing the Almighty. Hence, if we desire to be excellent, He will open our eyes, He will give us wisdom on what we need to do in specific situations.

A lot of believers are unattractive to unbelievers because some believers have little to admire in their lives. Unbelievers see we live just the same kind of life they live. They see the way we do things and they are just not attracted. It's time to begin to excel. Believers are meant to set the standard. Jesus did in his day. When will you start setting the standard?

Dave Hopla was a basketball star, he once made 78 NBA 3-pointers in a row without a miss. Overall Hopla makes more than 98% of the shots he takes and he now coaches basketball at a camp.

He said a lot of children nowadays don't excel as much as before because they don't want to put in the work and they don't practice enough.

At a 2007 camp in Los Angeles for example, he made all 272 basketball shots he took. He said there's nothing special about him, he just learned the skill. Hopla said "If you want to be the greatest shooter in the world, there are two things you have to do,

1. Shoot the ball correctly with correct shooting form.
2. Shoot it more than anybody else.

What he is saying is practice the skill and become the best. Excellence involves practicing your skill until it is sharpened to a notch above others.

Excellence is a virtue that cannot be ignored. When you see it, you just have to acknowledge it. Daniel was a man in the Bible that had a spirit of excellence upon him. He was different not by how he looked, but by what he did and who his God was. *Daniel 6:3*

Daniel was not a popular man when he was brought to Babylon but he kept his faith even when it was hard. He chose to not mix with the crowd. Daniel did not care what the consequences were. Time after time when pressure came he spoke up.

The first time was when he was asked to eat the king's meat. A second time when he was asked to intepret the king's dreams. A third time when he was put in the fiery furnace,

He always put his faith first and because of that God caused him to be distinguished he also put an excellent spirit upon him and he gave him great ability.

There are things you can do in the natural and there are things you can only do when God adds his ability to it. Then it becomes supernatural. Daniel did his best every time. God saw this and rewarded him and God was glorified in it too. When you desire to do your best and be your best without compromising your faith, God will always reward you because he knows he can trust you. Do you desire God to bless you with an excellent spirit, begin to do your best and be your best, go beyond the "normal" and don't compromise your faith. At school, at work, at church and in your everyday life.

Going beyond the normal signifies diligence and excellence. It is time to put all your efforts in all your endeavours. It's time to stand out and let be God be glorified in every area of our lives.

Excellence = your hard work, over and above what is required.

Excellence in action

"Once you deliver excellence with innovation and passion, it doesn't matter the color of your skin,. You will stand before kings."
Kunbi Adeoye, Founder - SESEWA

From an Interview with WOMEN OF RUBIES May 07, 2016

Kunbi is the executive director of SESEWA; a company she founded while still in university in 2009. She holds an LLB from Obafemi Awolowo University and was enrolled as a solicitor and advocate of the Supreme Court of Nigeria in 2010. Her company, SESEWA is at the forefront of providing internship and career opportunities for Nigeria's young generation and she is building a legacy for internship businesses in Nigeria. Adekunbi is a frequent speaker at youth events, and a big inspiration for young people in Africa cities in Africa. In this interview, the beautiful entrepreneur opens up on how she has been able to build SESEWA into a formidable brand .

Growing Up
Growing up for me was fun and filled with lessons. I was the child that was born to work.... I was really enterprising, I still am but when I was younger, I engaged in several kinds of businesses. I was particularly thrilled by the reward and satisfaction I got when I delivered a certain value or sold something. Let's just say I was born for enterprise!

Inspiration behind Sesewa?
My SESEWA experience is one that has changed my life forever.

For me, SESEWA is not just a business idea; it is more like a mandate attached to my life. It is seated at the core of my existence. SESEWA started first with my deepest desire to have people experience clarity and pursue a career they were really in love with because that was what I felt like after I had an internship in a law firm as an undergraduate. That experience left me empowered and I felt everyone deserved this opportunity- To be sure about what they wanted to create with their lives. This desire grew into a business because of my highly entrepreneurial spirit. The business operates as a social enterprise designed to tackle the diversified problems of recruitment and unemployment in Nigeria.

We specialize in providing internship, volunteering and job-shadowing opportunities to youths. With our well-developed curriculum, training school and set of assessments, the regular Nigerian graduate is transformed into a job-ready professional. This serves a dual purpose, in that it also provides organizations the best wave of talents to drive their corporate vision. For those who don't know, the name SESEWA is a coinage gotten from a Yoruba expression 'Se ise wa?' (Is there a Job?) This seems to be question on the lips of many Nigerian graduates and SESEWA will always say YES! We have got the RIGHT JOB for you!

Beyond Expectation
The truth remains that the big picture for SESEWA keeps expanding as we break new grounds; and yes! SESEWA is having the effect I caught a glimpse of in my mind years back. It just keeps getting better. Today, young people walk into my office with potentials that are worked upon and made valuable. They always leave better than they came. I have my interns go to clients and I get feedbacks from clients saying the interns are so fantastic that it is difficult to pick just one intern for the job. We call it the SESEWA Experience... As I will always say, "there is no discrimination against excellence." Once you deliver excellence with innovation and passion, it

doesn't matter the color of your skin, you will stand before kings.

Reception

Just like every other 'new' idea, SESEWA had some acceptance issues, basically because the concept was not so popular when we started. We just did our part, defined the value we were offering and we were determined to be the best at it. It wasn't long before individuals and organizations started warming up to the idea.

Let me mention here that there are times you just need to believe in you enough to give others the right reasons to believe in you too. I had people who believed in SESEWA because of the confidence and passion with which I spoke about the value we proposed to deliver even though we were doing it for the first time. I look back now; I am so fulfilled and grateful to God for being my Anchor.

Giving Up

This is one truth not so many people talk about. Fulfilling purpose is not as easy as spelling P.U.R.P.O.S.E. It sometimes feels like swimming against the current, it is super difficult. There were days that didn't look so bright, there were days I didn't feel up to the title "Executive Director" but at such times I was reminded of the WHY behind SESEWA and I got energized again.

This is one thing I tell everyone who cares to

listen, understand the purpose behind anything you do because when the road gets rough, you will be in one piece, strengthened by WHY you started in the first place. So, at the times I felt like giving up, I remembered SESEWA is not about me. This makes me jump out bed every morning whether I felt like it or not. Though right now, I feel we have gone too far to look back.

The only RIGHT way is FORWARD! in building a FAMILY. It is not just a work relationship. Our lives are so intertwined with the entire process that after the internship, it is hard to go back as just regular people. For the SESEWA family, we are consciously raising a new breed of excellent, talented professionals to redefine work in this part of the world.

Challenges

Every idea, business and journey has peculiar challenges. SESEWA had the challenge of acceptance as certain organizations didn't understand what we were proposing at first. We had to work on our product, curriculum to ensure we deliver excellent value every time.

We were also faced with fund challenges just as many start-ups with bills rising and demanding attention.

Future Plans For SESEWA

We hope to expand our sphere of influence, reach out to more youths, develop more products and programs that can come in handy to youths as we groom the best waves of talent, the most sought after in the land. We also hope to establish solid local and international partnerships with other organizations.

Advice for Young Unemployed Female Graduates?

Give yourself more credit. You are awesome too if only you can believe in yourself. Please don't define your entire life by your current phase of being without a job; just don't be idle. Keep your hands and mind busy. Get as much skills as possible. The internet has made it so easy for you to learn practically anything, enroll for online courses, volunteer for projects, get an internship just ensure you are increasing in value. What employers pay for is not the number of years you spent in school or the kind of school you graduated from but the value you can bring to the table.

For those who want to run their businesses, don't get too excited yet; get the needed skills and knowledge and please get a mentor! The concept of mentorship has been abused but I am sure you can still find great people who will be willing to take you through the paths they have walked in smarter ways.

What Makes You a Woman of Rubies?

I will just describe who I am in my own words and you will decide if that qualifies me to be a 'Woman of Rubies', I am simply Adekunbi Adeoye, a woman passionate about living out the blueprint of the Master for her life. I love God with my whole being. The process of fulfilling my purpose of helping others discover who they are has developed traits in me that I find amazing myself. I am a fantastic problem solver. I don't see problems; I see opportunities to touch lives. I am highly enterprising, I am so gifted that I believe I can sell anything even sand and still create a lucrative business out of it.

Final Word For Young Women?

Don't put a pause on your life waiting for anything! It doesn't suggest that you shouldn't be patient; just don't be mediocre. Discover what your life was designed to be and spend every moment living it out. Live freely! Dance, Sing out loud! You are beautiful, celebrate yourself always and quit settling for less!

Log on to sesewa.org, to know more about Kunbi's innovation and how she is helping several young Nigerians build their career.

NOTES

CHAPTER 11

GRACE AND FAVOR -
"THE ICING ON THE CAKE"

Grace and favor are words that are synonyms. You can use them simultaneously or singularly. There are words that signify the "God" factor in a situation.

What exactly does the word "grace" mean? According to Merriam-Webster dictionary, the full definition of grace is defined as the following among other definitions.

1a. unmerited divine assistance given humans for their regeneration or sanctification.
 b. a virtue coming from God.
 c. a state of sanctification enjoyed through divine grace.

2a. APPROVAL, FAVOR < stayed in his good grace>
 b. archaic: MERCY, PARDON
 c. a special favor
 d. a disposition to an act or instance of kindness, courtesy or clemency.
 e. a temporary exemption

When the word "favor" according to dictionary. com is defined as:

1. Something done or granted out of goodwill, rather than from justice or from remuneration ; a kind act. "to ask a favor"
2. "Friendly or well -disposed regard; goodwill. "to win the favor of the king.
3. The state of being approved or held in regard: to be in favor of court; styles that are now in favor.
4. Excessive kindness or unfair partiality; preferential treatment." To treat some people with favor and others with neglect."
5. A gift bestowed as a token of goodwill, kind regard, love etc, as formerly upon a knight by his lady.

Grace and favor are bestowed upon us by God not because we are good or because we have always done things right. No... not at all. As both definitions state, his grace and favor are blessings we enjoy from God because he loves us. He shows us that he is God.

There are a lot of people that feel like they can never get to the top of their career because there are too many obstacles they have to face.

A lot of time, human beings tend to depend on self-effort alone to achieve greatness however self-effort, diligence and excellence are good, however the favor of God and His grace can take you further than you can evr get on your own.

Let's examine the story of Joseph for instance in *Gen 39-50.*

Gen 39:2a " But the Lord was with Joseph (though a slave) he was a successful and prosperous man" (AMP-vs. 3)

"And his master saw that the lord was with him and that the lord made all that he did to flourish and succeed in his hand." vs.4a.

"So Joseph pleased (Potiphar) and found favor in his sight" vs5b

"The Lord blessed the Egyptian's house for Joseph's sake and the Lord's blessing was on all that he had in the house and in the field" vs. 21"

"But the Lord was with Joseph and showed him mercy and loving-kindness and gave him favor in the sight of the warden of the prison.

Vs 23b "For the Lord was with him and made whatever he did to prosper."

We can see that God was with him all the way. He made Joseph stand out, he gave him favor before his superiors. That is what God is able to do in your life and in my life.

No matter what you are going through, his grace is always sufficient for you.(*2nd Cor. 12:9* NKJV)

A lot of times, situations look like they are going to swallow us up, however we must always remember that with God's grace (His strength), we are able to go through those situations and come out victorious.

I have been talking about discovering, developing and deploying your gifts throughout this book.

And the part you have you have to play in getting to your place of prominence. There is however a part that you can't play, it's the part that grace and favor play in the life of a person.

When you play the natural part, God brings in the "super" to make it supernatural.

The supernatural is something you can never explain or never seem to understand. That is exactly what he did in Joseph's life. People around Joseph would have wondered why even while in the prison, he was still successful. The bible tells us, it was because God was with him.

When God is with you, whatever you do will prosper and as you do you your part, ensure to remember that God's part is equally important.

An example of "A Gift flavoured by Grace and Favor."

Singer Frank Edwards

FULL NAME: Frank Ugochukwu Edwards

DATE OF BIRTH: July 22, 1990

OCCUPATION: Singer: Gospel:Christian Hip hop, urban contemporary gospel

MARITAL STATUS: Not Married

Early Life and Background

Mr. Edwards was born into a family of seven. His birth name is Frank Ugochukwu Edwards. He was born in Enugu state, Nigeria.

Richboy as he's famously known, has been a blessing to the Christian world. Franklin portrayed interest in music right from childhood At the age of 7 he played the piano at home. Through the years, he grew through the ranks, perfecting his finger skills and now he plays on one of the world's largest stages.

Franklin Edwards is a dedicated member of Believers Love World Inc., A.k.a. Christ Embassy church where he is the pianist to the great minister of the gospel Pastor Chris Oyakhilome PHd. This great artist was raised, tutored, and mentored by Pastor Chris Oyakhilome,whom Frank holds in exceedingly, great esteem.

He believes Pastor Chris actually inspired him to do what he is doing today. He never dreamt of singing. He always wanted to be a pilot. He just found himself doing music because his pastor sings as well. He had earlier worked with other Gospel artist like Buchi, Sinach, and Samsong in production.

Here is what he said when he was asked how he became successful.

"It is grace, because, before my first album came out, I never stood in front of two people to sing not to talk of the whole church, I never held the microphone in the church to lead the choir in the choir rehearsal not to talk of Sunday service, not even Wednesday service, nobody gave me that opportunity, but I was working underground, just recording my songs and when I was recording these songs I was not recording it for album, I was just trying out some of this things I suggested to people and they rejected so I was just trying them out myself, I didn't plan to make an album, but you know how it is, people hear one song, it is nice, record another one and I did, before you know it the songs that I recorded got to Pastor Chris' table,

I did not even know about it, we were having a global service it was December 31st night and I was there as a keyboardist sitting down when Pastor Chris came out preaching. Then he walked towards me and whispered to me, "Your song that I heard, are you ready to sing it now?"

My heart just flew because I had never held a microphone in the church before and here I am, being asked to sing to the whole world. I just started sweating immediately, I didn't know when I nodded my head to say yes, I think my head moved on its own. Then he asked if the sound department had my soundtrack and I said I don't know. He sent someone to go and ask, and I was just hoping that they should say they don't have it and the guy came back saying they have it!

He gave me the microphone, the first time anybody gave me a microphone to sing in front of the whole world. I had not started going for programs. I was still in the studio just doing my thing. So I held the microphone and started singing, I didn't know what took over me, I watched the video after the program. People lifted their hands up, people were on the floor.

Even pastor was singing it word for word which means he had been listening to it. Fom that night in fact, my facebook page was jammed and the story has not been the same. That was my turning point."

Career and Life

His debut album *The Definition* was released in 2008. It was 14 track album and was distributed by Honesty Music. Angels on the Runway his second album was released in 2010 and another one Unlimited in 2011.

He rose to fame by Divine Intervention or should I say he was in the right place at the right time doing the right thing as expected of him. Today he has numerous hit songs that have continued to enjoy massive airplay in churches and beyond Nigeria shore. Some of his songs includes, You too dey bless me o, Omema o, Mma Mma, Welcome to Zion and much more. He is a role model and inspiration to the youths.

Producing his songs under his world class Record Label, christened "ROCKTOWN", the young multi-talented artist and motivational speaker has been celebrated for revolutionalizing Nigerian Gospel Music, introducing a new and exiting twist, with his new blend of rock, fused with a little pop and fuji.

His debut album *The Definition* was released in 2008. It was a 14-track album and was distributed by Honesty Music.[2] *Angels on the Runway* his second album was released in 2010 and another, *Unlimited,* in 2011. *Tagjam*, was released in November 2011. He is currently known as Nigeria's Hottest Gospel rock artist in Nigeria. In 2013 he he appeared in the live performance of Sinach's *"I know who I am"* video. Besides being an artist with many songs in all musical genre, He is also a genius producer, master mixer. As a result, Rock Town Records, which he owns, has a generation of up and coming talent with names like GIL, Divyn, David and many others.

His 3rd and 4th album are all critically acclaimed success. They are impressive work that will stand the times. They have also been widely sold across Nigeria and beyond and is still selling out fast in stores. The follow up concert video has also been raking up sales ever since its release.

He is also credited with various nominations including The NEA Awards 2009, and also The Nigerian Gospel Awards 2012, where he merited six different nominations. In the aftermath of over seven years of making global impact with soul lifting, earth shaking gospel music, the best of Frank Edwards is still to come.

This Nigerian born music minister was the winner

of the Nigerian Gospel Awards (Rock Artist Of The Year) 2010, he also had a graceful outing at the African Gospel Awards 2012, where he won the Best Gospel Artist West Africa Award. Recently also, his song "Superstar No.1" bagged the Loveworld Awards Hit Song Of The Year 2012, and was awarded $10,000.

He has also been performing within and outside Nigeria ever since the work was put out.

The singer is said to have a collaboration with gospel music legend Don Moen in year 2015.

Awards

Frank is an artist who has won a lot of popular and unpopular awards.

He won the award of the best Gospel Rock artiste in the first annual awards.

He also won west Africa best male vocalist in 2012/ best hit single at the love world awards 2012/ and 3 awards at the Nigeria gospel music awards (male artiste of the year,song of the year and best male vocal)

- See more at: http://www.takemetonaija.com/2015/05/singer-frank-edwards-full-biogaphylife.html#sthash.LkaG1lor.dpuf

CHAPTER 12

MODERN DAY EXAMPLES DEPOLYMENT... PROMINENCE

It is necessary to look at some people in our world who have discovered developed and deployed their gifts effectively. Looking at these few examples is necessary to encourage you and I and remind us that each person has gifts that he/she may be neglecting or not using to full capacity.

1. Usain St Leo, Bolt

Sprinter Usain Bolt is arguably the fastest man in the world, winning three gold medals at the 2008 Olympic Games in Beijing, China, and becoming the first man in Olympic history to win both the 100-meter and 200-meter races in record times. Bolt won his fourth Olympic gold medal in the men's 100-meter race at the 2012 Summer Olympic Games in London, beating rival Yohan Blake, who took silver. Bolt ran the race in 9.63 seconds, a new Olympic record, making him the first man in history to set three world records in a single Olympic Games competition. The win marked Bolt's second consecutive gold medal in the 100. Bolt went on to compete in the men's 200, claiming his second consecutive gold medal in that race. He is the first man to win both the 100 and 200 at consecutive Olympic Games, as well as the first man to ever win back-to-back gold medals in double sprint

Background

Usain Bolt was born in Jamaica on August 21, 1986. Both a standout cricket player and a sprinter early on, Bolt's natural speed was noticed by coaches at school, and he began to focus solely on sprinting under the tutelage of Pablo McNeil, a former Olympic

sprint athlete. (Glen Mills would later serve as Bolt's coach and mentor.) As early as age 14, Bolt was wowing fans of sprinting with his lightning speed, and he won his first high school championships medal in 2001, taking the silver in the 200-meter race.

At the age of 15, Bolt took his first shot at success on the world stage at the 2002 World Junior Championships in Kingston, Jamaica, where he won the 200-meter dash, making him the youngest world-junior gold medalist ever. Bolt's feats impressed the athletics world, and he received the International Association of Athletics Foundation's Rising Star Award that year and soon was given the apt nickname "Lightning Bolt."

Professional Career

Despite a nagging hamstring injury, Bolt was chosen for the Jamaican Olympic squad for the 2004 Athens Olympics. He was eliminated in the first round of the 200-meter, though, again hampered by injury.

Bolt reached the world Top 5 rankings in 2005 and 2006. Unfortunately, injuries continued to plague the sprinter, preventing him from completing a full professional season.

The year 2007 proved to be a breakthrough one for Bolt, as he broke the national 200-meter record held for over 30 years by Donald Quarrie, and earned two silver medals at the World Championship in

Osaka, Japan. These medals boosted Bolt's desire to run, and he took a more serious stance toward his career.

Olympic Gold and World Records

Bolt announced that he would run the 100-meter and 200-meter events at the Beijing Summer Olympics in 2008. In the 100-meter final, bolt broke the world record, winning in 9.69 seconds. Not only was the record set without a favorable wind, but he also visibly slowed down to celebrate before he finished (and his shoelace was untied), an act that aroused much controversy later on.

At the 2012 Summer Olympic Games, held in London, bolt won his fourth Olympic gold medal in the men's 100-meter race, beating rival Yohan Blake, who won silver in the event. Bolt ran the race in 9.63 seconds, a new Olympic record. The win marked Bolt's second consecutive gold medal in the 100. He went on to compete in the men's 200, claiming his second consecutive gold medal in that race. He is the first man to win both the 100 and 200 in consecutive Olympic Games, as well as the first man to ever win triple gold medals in double sprints and the 4x 100m relay races.. Bolt's accomplishments have made him the first man in history to set three world records in a single Olympic Games competition.

Accolades and 'Lightning' Pose

Following his 200 meters, in an interview with CBS News, bolt detailed his pride over his 2012 performance: "It's what I came here to do. I'm now a legend. I'm also the greatest athlete to live. I've got nothing left to prove." Bolt took back the 100-meter world title on August 11, 2013, after having lost the title in 2011. Although Bolt didn't strike his signature "lightning bolt" pose after the race, his winning image still caused a stir, with lightning striking just as he crossed the finish line.

In 2015, Bolt faced some challenges. He came in second at the Nassau IAAF World Relays in May, but secured an individual win in the 200-meter event at Ostrava Golden Spike event that same month. He also dominated the 200-meter race at the New York Addias Grand Prix that June. But trouble with his pelvic muscles led him to withdraw from two races. Bolt, however, made a comeback that July with a 100-meter win at London's Anniversary Games. Still this elite runner is expected to face some stiff competition from American Justin Gatlin at the 2015 World Championships.

Bolt's achievements in sprinting have earned him numerous awards, including the IAAF World Athlete of the Year (twice), Track & Field Athlete of the Year and Laureus Sportsman of the Year.

2016 Summer Olympics in Brazil

Usain Bolt crossed the line in 19.78sec.
Photograph: Lucy Nicholson/Reuters

"Moments after Usain Bolt had clinched his eighth Olympic title with much the same ease as his other seven, he smiled serenely into the cameras and hollered: "Number one!" Once again, he had proven that he was the greatest sprinter in history. But, perhaps for the first time, there was something else: a sense that as he approaches his 30th birthday on Sunday, he is not quite able to hit the very highest notes as he once did.

Of course Bolt was still far too good for this field. He made a whip-sharp start and had established a lead of three or four metres by the bend. The rest was just noise – and poise – as he came home in

19.78sec. It was a season's best time but also the slowest 200m he has run in a major championship final since 2008. Perhaps he was right to say that he would only be running the 100m at the world championships in London next year.

The Jamaican's face as he crossed the line told you he expected to be quicker. Last year in Beijing he had run 19.55sec, off nowhere near as good a winter, and two days ago had even floated the possibility of breaking his own world record of 19.19, set in Berlin in 2009. That wasn't to be, but victory – as usual provided more than adequate compensation.

St Bolt wins in Rio again, Ashton and Jones also take gold

"I am getting older, I am not as young and fresh, but I am excited I got the gold, and that is the key thing," he admitted. "I focus on what I need to do because if I don't there will not be a Usain Bolt. The fact I came here and everything worked out it is a brilliant feeling."

At the press conference afterwards Bolt was asked whether he was angry at the finish. "I was disappointed," he replied. "Always happy to win and wanted to run faster even if didn't break world record. Thanks to de Grasse my legs were tired. My legs wouldn't respond in the final. I'm getting older so don't recover like I usually do. The key thing is I won which is what I came to do."

"My legs just didn't feel fresh. I'm not 26 anymore. I'm not 21 anymore. It's not as easy as it used to be.

I wanted it but my body couldn't take it. The elements may have made a little bit of a difference."

When asked whether this was his last 200m, he dangled the possibility of a U-turn, but his reaction suggested that was it. "I don't know," he replied. "I said when I come to the championships in London next year it would be 100m and that's it. My coach has a way of trying to convince me, but personally I believe this is my last one."

The nearest man to Bolt was the Canadian Andre De Grasse, who took silver in a modest 20.02 – nearly a quarter of a second slower than he had run in the semi-finals. During that race De Grasse had showed enough speed to catch, and then hold, a conversation with Bolt as they crossed the line. Such was the gap in the final, however, that he would have needed a megaphone to be heard.

Behind him an almighty battle was raging for bronze. For all the world it looked like Britain's Adam Gemili was going to win it, but he perhaps dipped a tiny bit too early and found himself pipped on the line by the Frenchman Christophe Lemaitre. To add to the 22-year-old Gemili's pain he was given the same time as Lemaitre, 20.12 sec. Understandably he was heartbroken.

"I'm just heartbroken," admitted Gemili. "I put so much into that run and to get so close is just absolutely gutted. I was on the inside and I knew Bolt would go and a lot of people would try and go with him. But fourth place is probably the worst place you can be. I've got no words. We're not here to fill lanes any more. We've got guys who can make these finals and push.

Meanwhile Bolt was off, accepting the dreamy love and cheers of the crowd. The result meant that he has won every Olympic and world title over 200m since 2008. But there is another statistic that shows his dominance in his favourite event. Since the start of 2008, he has run exactly 50 races in over 200m. And only twice has he lost – in the heats of the 2008 Olympics in Beijing, when he strolled around the track and allowed the Trinidad and Tobago athlete Rondell Sorrillo to beat him, and at the 2012 Jamaican trials where Yohan Blake pipped him to the post.

Despite not being at his best here, that record was never in doubt."

Written by Sean Ingle, The Guardian

https://www.theguardian.com/sport/2016/aug/18/usain-bolt-jamaica-200m-gold-medal-olympic-rio-2016

2. Joyce Meyer

Joyce Meyer was born on 4ᵗʰ June 1943 in St Louis, Missouri, USA. She is one of the world's leading Bible teachers and speakers who has her own syndicated television and radio program called *"Enjoying Everyday Life"*. She is the leader of Joyce Meyer Ministries worldwide. She is a New York Times bestselling author, and her books have helped millions of people find hope and restoration through Jesus Christ. She also has a magazine titled *"Enjoying Everyday Life."*

Joyce started as a local Bible teacher in 1976, then became an associate pastor of a church in St. Louis, Missouri in 1980. She became an ordained minister in 1981. In 1985 her ministry was titled *"Life in the Word"*.

By 2003, Joyce's ministry grew by leaps and bounds and soon she was teaching citywide, statewide, countrywide and now worldwide through Joyce Meyer Ministries and her television, radio and magazine titles were changed to *"Enjoying Everyday Life."* She teaches on hundreds of subjects based on her experience and how she applies the Bible to every facet of her life.

Joyce holds an earned PhD in theology from Life Christian University in Tampa, Florida, an honorary doctorate in Divinity from Oral Roberts University in Tulsa, Oklahoma, and an honorary doctorate in Sacred Theology from Grand Canyon University in Phoenix, Arizona.

Joyce has authored over 90 self-help non-fiction books and a handful of fiction books.

Joyce Meyer is a woman I highly admire because she has shown the world that with God on your side, you can overcome every challenge that seeks to stop you in life. She is a woman that loved to talk and she has been able to harness and turn that gift of talking into teaching other people. She also shows that God can ensure your mess will become your message.

3. Oprah Winfrey

Oprah Winfrey was born Orpah Gail Winfrey on 29th January 1954, in Kosciusko, Mississippi, to Vernita Lee, a former maid, and Vernon Winfrey, a coal miner, barber, and city councilman.

While Winfrey has been cited as the richest African American of the 20th century, she does not come from a rich, or even middle class, family. She was born in an economically troubled neighborhood and raised by a single-teenaged mother in the city of Milwaukee. Orpah, named after a biblical character, had a name no one could pronounce, so her family and friends starting calling her Oprah. Shortly after Oprah's birth, Vernita Lee left her daughter and traveled north. Oprah was then raised by her grandmother, Hatti Mae Lee. Oprah while being raised by her grandmother lived in terrible conditions. Oprah's only friends were farm animals, however even at that age Oprah had a very imaginative mind. Oprah would frequently give the animals dramatic parts and included them in games. This was perhaps where she had gotten the craze for acting, and would soon be seen in legendary masterpieces such as *The Color Purple*(1985). Oprah because of her grandmother's values, had religion and God instilled in herself at a very young age. Oprah because of her grandmother knew how to read, and write before the age of three. Oprah during church would recite poems, and verses from the bible. Soon the church, and the entire neighborhood knew she had a gift and was nicknamed, "The Little Speaker". This would soon prompt her to become a woman with a strong perspective, which millions across the world would want to have insight on. This prepared her for *The Oprah Winfrey Show* (1986).

Due to her ability to read and write before the age of three, when enrolled in school she was often promoted several grades ahead of her age. Oprah at the age of six went to live with her mother, Vernita Lee. Vernita worked as a maid, so Oprah was often left alone at home with her cousins. Oprah due to her busy mother was paid little attention to at home, this is what prompted Oprah to started misbehaving and talking back to her mother. Vernita Lee then decided it was best Oprah live with her father in Nashville Tennessee. Oprah while living in Tennessee, found out her mother was pregnant and her mother requested for her to come back to Milwaukee to live with her mother and half-sister. When Oprah was nine she was raped by her nineteen year old cousin who was babysitting her. This wouldn't be the only time she was sexually abused she would then be sexually abused by her cousin, a family friend, her mother's boyfriend, and her uncle during her stay in Milwaukee. Toward all these incidents, she never told a soul because the predators swore her to silence. At the age of thirteen Oprah ran away from home, this was due to her years of abuse and at the age of fourteen she became pregnant with an ill son who died shortly after birth. Oprah took the death of her son as she was given a second chance in life. Oprah's mother sent her to live once again with her father in Nashville, Tennessee. Oprah's father was very strict and made education the number-one priority for Oprah.

Oprah attended Nashville East High School. Oprah during high-school wasn't precisely certain toward what she wanted to do, however she knew it was something with speaking or drama. Oprah was also elected school president and met with president Richard being a part of public speaking classes in her high-school.

Oprah during the last year of high-school was rehearsing with her drama class when a local radio station, WVOL spotted her and asked her if she would like to read on radio. Oprah was then given a job reading the news on the radio. Oprah soon entered into a public speaking contest where the grand prize was a scholarship to Tennessee State University. Oprah won the contest and received a scholarship to Tennessee State University where she majored in Speech Communications and Performing Arts.

Oprah during her college education was offered a job as a co-anchor on the CBS television station, she declined several times before she was convinced by her speech professor that it may be the ultimate step to launch her career. Oprah wanted to find work outside of Nashville Tennessee and was soon offered a job in Baltimore, Maryland. The job offers came up a few months before her graduation, she had to choose between the job and graduating, so she decided to choose the job in Maryland as the offer was very tempting. At the job in Maryland she wasn't a very good reporter and was shortly fired. Oprah's boss set her up as a talk show host on a morning talk show called, People (1978). Immediately after the first show Oprah knew this is what she wanted to do for the rest of her life. Oprah strengthened the talk show for seven years and then she decided it was time to move on.

In 1981 Oprah sent recorded tapes of the show to a talk-show in Chicago called A.M. Chicago. They immediately offered her the job and in September of 1985 she changed the name of the show to, "The Oprah Winfrey Show". The first broadcast of The Oprah Winfrey Show was on September 8,1986 it broadcast nationally. The Oprah Winfrey show first targeted woman, however soon due to controversial topics and intriguing topics Oprah brought on to the show it appealed to people of all genders ,ethnics ,and ages. Oprah promoted many things on her show such as books, movie releases all of which people were eager to know what her opinions were of them. Oprah helped broaden not just woman's point of view and significance but Oprah helped to realize that every human has an importance in this world. From it's first broadcast The Oprah Winfrey show went on to receive multiple Day Time Emmy Awards and several other prestigious awards. Winfrey expanded the Oprah Winfrey show and started releasing a monthly magazine which was called, O: The Oprah Magazine. The first issue was in 2000. The series finale of the Oprah Winfrey Show as on its twenty-fifth season and it aired on May,25,2011. Concluding a segment of her career toward which she used as a device to inspire millions and help thousands to lead a better life.

Oprah's made her debut as a film actress in the 1985 period drama film, The Color Purple. Oprah played a troubled housewife named Sofia. Oprah was nominated for an Academy Award for Best Supporting Actress. This movie went on to become a Broadway musical adaptation. In 1998 Oprah starred in the movie, Beloved which she also produced. Winfrey played the character Seethe who was a former slave. Winfrey has also acted in several movies such as Charlotte's Web (2006), Bee Movie (2007), and The Princess and the Frog (2009).

Oprah Winfrey in 1998 received an Achievement Award from the National Academy of Television Arts and Sciences. In 2011 Oprah Winfrey received a Jean Hersholt Humanitarian Award from the Academy Of Motion Pictures Arts And Sciences.

Oprah Winfrey will forever be remembered as an innovator through the landmarks she made, becoming the first African American to host a television show. Inspiring millions of people across the world, discussing significant issues on her show such as equal rights toward genders, racism, poverty, and many others. Oprah will be seen as an icon someone who paved the way for others to become successful.

- IMDb Mini Biography by: Peter Sean

4. Interview: Meet Ifeoma Adefemi "Iposhlooks," the former mechanical engineer who turned an albino into a superstar with a makeover.

From an Interview with **Women of Rubies**
May 14, 2016

Ifeoma Adefemi's story reads like a scene in a drama. It is strange but true. She is a mechanical engineering graduate from the University of Ado Ekiti who is one of the leading lights in Nigeria's beauty industry. She gained wide acclaim when she gave an albino a makeover. Ify, as she is often called by her clients is the CEO of Iposh looks, a fledging makeup artistry business. In this interview she reveals what makes her unique, why she embarked on that famed makeover for Chinwe and lot's more.

Ifeoma…the brain behind *iposh looks*

I am Ifeoma Adefemi, from Anambra state, Nigeria. I was born and bred in the south west. I am married with a son and the CEO of Iposh looks. I am the only girl amongst 3 boys. I think I grew up fast because the responsibilities of being a first born did not allow me do the "sand" play for long. Those days, my mum used to say I was very ugly and that my brothers where finer, so I was forced to enhance my looks. It all started from there.

Discovering my passion for makeup artistry

I started Makeup artistry because my mum used to say I was very ugly. Because I did it well on myself, people started commending me for it. I enjoy it even more than engineering. I started giving it a thought and decided to make it a career.

Childhood preparations

I am an only girl with boys. I don't think my childhood prepared me for this. If I wasn't doing make-up I would be doing fashion designing or interior décor. I just love colours. Till now, I still have friends that are into fashion that I still give suggestions to.

Starting out in business

When I started out, it was just a hobby then I made it a business. Lives are hinging on Iposh looks. Even if something bad should happen to the business, my husband will be able to take care of the family, how about my team who are part of the dream. ? A lot of things inspire me to continue against all odds. It's the joy I derive when I see a bride smile in the mirror, that keeps me going.

The inspiration behind the brand name

I am a very playful person. My boyfriend of then who happens to be my husband, usually call me Ariel which happens to be a Greek word for lioness. So I initially chose the name Ariel concept, people where calling it Ariel (the detergent) so I opted for Iphy's flair. I consulted some of my friends on BBM telling them I wanted a new business name. One of them suggested Iposh. Those days iPhone was the rave of the moment. So I finally decided to go for Iposh.

Describing my personality

I think I am a blend of an extrovert and an introvert. Some people think I don't talk at all and some people think I talk a lot. For me, it's about where I am. I am very careful. Growing up with guys made me outspoken. Guys would push you to the extreme.

The Albino Makeover that went viral
My most memorable makeover

The most memorable makeover will still be the albino makeover I did. Its memorable not just because of its acceptance, but for me it was more about the motive. I was in a point in my makeover career when it just became boring. I just wanted something more. I wasn't going out scouting for an albino.

I was on my explore page on Instagram and I saw this albino girl who was on a trip to Obudu Cattle Ranch and she just had this bum short on. She lives life like she doesn't care. She loves herself and so I asked myself, "How can I encourage her, make her feel extremely good and also encourage others?"

I sent her a direct message telling her I was a big fan and offered her a makeup treat. I have never done makeup for an albino before, so for me I was taking up a challenge/making a damsel really happy. She was skeptical of the outcome and to be honest I was also scared. I was even afraid to upload it on my page, but I found the courage to, and I'm glad I did.

Afterwards, she sent me a message saying I made her touch lives. She has been getting calls from mothers with albino kids and she indeed feels the shoot was really more than just a shoot."

What makes Iposh Unique?

I will be able to answer that question based on what people have said. Some people have said they love the way we create our eyebrows, some also say they love the way I craft my post on Instagram even though I have stopped doing that lately because I have had a lot on my plate.

Ifeoma with her husband & son

Challenges

I didn't know whether to make her look like a yellow girl or to retain her albino look. I was confused. I had to ask her what she was comfortable in and to be fair, she said anything. I felt every other day she is an albino but she could just look different. So I gave her that tan look. It was something I won't do ordinarily. I just decided to do it. I also had a color challenge, choosing between red or any other color.

Advice to young women entrepreneurs

I am an advocate for pursuing one's passion. I didn't have to prepare for this interview, because it's something I live for. I can keep talking on and on. Recently, I had to pay a sum of money to a senior colleague to coach me on how I can get the best from my staff. Imagine if I am not passionate about my career. I advise female entrepreneurs to do something they enjoy. You will be frustrated if you are not passionate. I wasn't born in Lagos but marriage made me relocate to Lagos and getting new clients in Lagos was a major challenge.

For me it's about giving. There is something that giving does to me. My son can't give me that joy. I won't stop being relevant because I won't stop giving. I believe there is nothing I have that I wasn't given. Some of my colleagues tell me to draw back and not give all I know, but I insist on being a giver. I can't imagine a life without giving.

5. Meet Anuoluwapo Adebanjo, The Nigerian Woman who designed Queen Elizabeth's 90th Birthday cake

Top Nigerian baker, Anuoluwapo Adebanjo of Edible Spices bakery and events designed the 90th birthday cake for the British High Commission in Lagos. The cake, featured on several blogs with pictures of Nigerian celebrities and dignitaries had so many people asking: "Who designed it? A very excited and thankful Anu shared the story behind the cake and how she was contacted.

Her post as shared on her Facebook page:
"YOU are not man that YOU should lie…over 10

years ago, God gave me a dream bigger than my capacity, I have never tried to figure it out, I serve a great and mighty God, I just knew I had to wait for the right time… He told me I won't have to beg for it, neither will I pay my way to success (and my pride began, yes I'm proud.

I have the backing of the Greatest God) all I needed to do was just to rest and believe in his mighty words. I have been told severally to send cake samples to some celebrities for hype(yes it's good when you are building a brand) but I don't believe in it, I believe if my work is good enough, with God, kings, celebrities will sought after my brand not for self-pity (if I have to send to a top person I admire, I'll do with no strings attached, I do some anonymously anyways, you might be the next person..lol)

I have gotten several requests from media houses to pay for newspaper publications/Tv interviews so that I can be featured (it's good for business but I won't do that maybe for now). It has never been about fame and quick money (those who know me can testify) I believe in process.

I know God wants to take me through a part only him will take glory for… some people ask how can a self-taught cake maker be this good? Well I have told you severally I'm God taught, I don't rely on my own understanding, myself and the Holy Spirit hold hands when I'm working on a cake (this is my secret o trust me).

So I was contacted last week to make a cake for the Queen's Birthday Party, I had no idea what the design would be until yesterday evening… I was told dignitaries have been taking pictures of the cake at the British deputy high commissioner's residence, A great achievement! To God alone be the glory. I'm not where God wants me to be yet but I'm grateful I'm following through bitter-sweet process.

Happy 90th birthday to Her Royal Highness Queen Elizabeth ll."

#ediblespices #gratefultoGodforall
#heseestheheartandherewardsaccordingly". -May 2016

NOTES

CHAPTER 13

BIBLICAL EXAMPLES DEPLOYMENT... PROMINENCE

It is necessary to look at some people in the bible who have discovered developed and deployed their gifts. They did not find it easy but they were challenged by God and by people and they were able to see what gifts they had and how they could use them.

1. Gideon

Gideon was a young man who nobody reckoned with, he didn't feel like he had anything that would be useful to anybody, not even to himself. God however saw differently, God saw a man that had a gift of leadership and he only needed Gideon to be willing to surrender himself and his gifts to him.

Gideon could only see his own insufficiencies and weaknesses (as you can see from the conversation in *Judges 6: 13- 16*) that ensued between Gideon and God. Gideon tried to convince God that there had to be somebody else that was more capable than he was. Eventually he agreed that he would" save Israel from the hands of the Midianites" but he still needed God to convince him that it was going to be a worthwhile venture (*Judges 6 : 19-26, Judges 6; 36-40*).

Could this passage be speaking about you as well? What gift skill or talents do you have in your hands, in your heart, that you feel is not worth much? A lot of people don't see themselves the way God sees them. A lot of times, we tend to look outwards when we need the solutions to life's problems. Have you ever thought of looking inwards?

Gideon had a gift of leadership hidden inside but he was looking toward other people to deliver Israel. *Judges 6:34-35* states "the spirit of the Lord came upon Gideon then he blew the trumpet and the Abiezrites gathered behind him" He also sent messages to Asher, Zebulun, and Naphtali and they came up to meet them".

Wow... when Gideon decided to obey and use his gift, God backed him up. He however struggled with how to walk in his new role (Judges 6:36-40). This was expected and God reassured him and even gave him the strategies of how to go against the Midianites *Judges 7 : 1-25, 8:1-25.*

When you discover your gift, and decide to deploy into your world, you become a blessing to your world. You end up giving more than you envisaged you could. You however should not do it without God as your help as you can see that this was the key that helped Gideon in achieving all that he did.

2. The Wife of the sons of the Prophet (2nd Kings 4:1-7)

Here was a woman that her husband had just died, apparently the husband was a debtor while alive and since since he was now dead, the creditor was going to take his sons away to be slaves in order for the debt to be redeemed. How sad!

This woman was so distraught, she did not know what to do except cry out to Elisha the prophet, she did not think of looking inwards. When asked what she had she believed she didn't have anything.

Most of us will respond in the exact same way if we are asked that question. I don't have anything, we always tend to believe other people are gifted but not us, we believe other people have creative ideas but not us because we never look inwards. We are always looking outwards at other people.

Maybe it's time to do it self-examination what do you have in your house? What gifts talents skills do you have that God wants to use to take you to prominence. What assets do you have that the world is waiting for? What creative ideas do you have that you've refused to share with anyone? Your world is waiting.

Do you know that the woman said in 2nd Kings 4:2b "Your maidservant has nothing in the house but a jar of oil" (NKJV)?

Elisha was listening to her and as soon as he heard her say "But a Jar of oil", he knew that was enough for God to work with. He immediately gave her instructions on what to do with the oil (2nd Kings 4:3-6) As she followed the instructions, her prominence began to come, wealth began to come to where there was debt.

He gave her further instructions to ensure she was set free from debt forever. Instructions are very important if you are to use your gift efficiently and effectively.

Gideon listened to instructions from God and when he followed the strategies God gave him, he won the battle.

Action Time!

As discussed earlier, instructions could come from God, from prophets assigned to you or mentors/coaches. Aim to be like the wife of the sons of the prophet who also listened to instructions from the prophet and followed each one and this brought her to a place of prominence.

1. Are you ready to deploy your gift?
2. What do you need to do?
3. What instructions do you need to follow?
4. Stop Procrastinating... Start Today.

CONCLUSION

TYING IT ALL TOGETHER

Matthew 25:14-30 talks about the parable of the talent. It is a story that touches me deeply every time I read it because it causes me to stop and pause, it causes me to ask myself whether I am a good steward of all the gifts God has blessed me with. This includes spiritual, physical, financial and otherwise.

Parable of the Talents

[14] "For it is just like a man who was about to take a journey, and he called his servants together and entrusted them with his possessions. [15] To one he gave five [a]talents, to another, two, and to another, one, each according to his own ability; and then he went on his journey. [16] The one who had received the five talents went at once and traded with them, and he [made a profit and] gained five more. [17] Likewise the one who had two [made a profit and] gained two more. [18] But the one who had received the one went and dug a hole in the ground and hid his master's money.

¹⁹ "Now after a long time the master of those servants returned and settled accounts with them. ²⁰ And the one who had received the five talents came and brought him five more, saying, 'Master, you entrusted to me five talents. See, I have [made a profit and] gained five more talents.' ²¹ His master said to him, 'Well done, good and faithful servant. You have been faithful and trustworthy over a little, I will put you in charge of many things; share in the joy of your master.'

²² "Also the one who had the two talents came forward, saying, 'Master, you entrusted two talents to me. See, I have [made a profit and] gained two more talents.' ²³ His master said to him, 'Well done, good and faithful servant. You have been faithful and trustworthy over a little, I will put you in charge of many things; share in the joy of your master.'

²⁴ "The one who had received one talent also came forward, saying, 'Master, I knew you to be a harsh and demanding man, reaping [the harvest] where you did not sow and gathering where you did not scatter seed. ²⁵ So I was afraid [to lose the talent], and I went and hid your talent in the ground. See, you have what is your own.'

²⁶ "But his master answered him, 'You wicked, lazy servant, you knew that I reap [the harvest] where I did not sow and gather where I did not scatter seed. ²⁷ Then you ought to have put my money with the bankers, and at my return I would have received my money back with interest.²⁸ So take the talent away from him, and give it to the one who has the ten talents.'

²⁹ "For to everyone who has [and values his blessings and gifts from God, and has used them wisely], more will be given, and [he will be richly supplied so that] he will have an abundance; but from the one who does not have [because he has ignored or disregarded his blessings and gifts from

God], even what he does have will be taken away. [30] And throw out the worthless servant into the outer darkness; in that place[of grief and torment] there will be weeping [over sorrow and pain] and grinding of teeth [over distress and anger:" *Matthew 25:14- 30* [Amp]

As we seek to tie all the knots together in this book, I will like you to take a good look at your life and ask yourself if you have been a good steward of all the blessings abounding in your life.

A steward is a person who manages or looks after another person's property. You may wonder, what property am I required to take care of... hmm? Those gifts of yours (cooking, writing, baking, the gift of administration, digital media, event planning, making people laugh and acting, etc.

Whatever gift you have is a blessing that God has given you and he expects you to use it to the best of your ability. Remember, there is a day coming when you will have to give account of all the gifts you were given. Will you be found to be a good steward or a bad steward?

You have seen examples of people in this book that have been good stewards of the talents that were bestowed on them. What about you? The world is waiting for your gifts to manifest. If your gift has manifested, do not stop there. Do everything you can to be the best you can be. The sky is not the limit, it's only the beginning. It's time to walk into your place of prominence.

In the story of the talents, there was a difference that was evident between the good and the bad stewards. The first 2 servants went about "quickly" to make more out of what was given to them, the 3rd servant went and buried his talent.

We see what the 3rd servant said in his statement

" So I was afraid, and I went and hid your talent in the ground" *Matthew 25:25a*

He let fear rob him of what he had and he ended up losing everything.

When you look at your own life, are you letting fear stop you:
- fear of the unknown,
- fear of failing,
- fear of stepping out,
- fear of people laughing at you,
- fear of being criticized,
- fear of being judged,
- fear of making sacrifices or
- fear of the hard work involved.

I might not have mentioned your fear but whatever it may be, you know it and you have to choose to not let it rob you of the greater things that have been planned for your life.

I want to leave you with this last word : It's time to begin to do more than what you have been doing. If you have not been doing anything, it's time to rise up.

Refuse to let anything stop you from reaching your goals.

Let this book be a challenge to you to move you to the next level in your life.

I will be waiting to hear from you of all the wonderful feats you have been able to conquer.

END NOTES

Discover

Noah Websters '1828 Dictionary (online version)
Imagine Big by Terri Savelle Foy

Scripture verses from:

The Message Bible
New King James version-1979, 1980, 1982, 1990 by
Thomas Nelson Inc.
New Century version
MOM'S BIBLE, GOD'S WISDOM FOR MOTHERS
2010 BY Barbara .J.Wolgemuth
Published in Nashville, TN, Thomas Nelson Inc.
The Living Bible
The Everyday Life Bible (containing the Amplified
Old Testament and Amplified New Testament)
Notes and Commentary by Joyce Meyer
New International Version

The Power of a Praying Woman Bible by Stormie
Omartian

Develop

Definitions of Develop
www.webstersdictionary1828.com
www.businessdictionary.com/definition/
preparation.html
www.mirriam-webster.com

Scripture verses from:

The Message Bible
New Living Translation
New King James version
New Century version

Deploy

Make your own at Electricfairground.com
Fitnessquotes.net
New King James version
dictionary.cambridge.org

A Place of Prominence

free dictionary.com
Leveraging for success by Pastor Matthew Ashimolowo
New Living Translation
The Message Bible
Article on Dave Hopla (usab.com)
www.sesewa.org

Frank Edwards Biography
-www.takemetonaija.com/2015/05/singer-frank
Edwards – full bibiography

Usain Bolt's image
www.independent.co.uk

Oprah Winfrey's image
(50 things you didn't know about Oprah Winfrey)
www.boomsbeat.com
IMDB Mini biography by Peter Sean

Joyce Meyer image
Joyce Meyer: Why do we often avoid prayer?
www.christiantoday.com

Ifeoma Adefemi
women of rubies.com/categories/interviews
www.women of rubies.com/interviews

Anuoluwapo Adebanjo
Edible spices/facebook
w w w . f a c e b o o k . c o m > P l a c e s > L a g o s ,
Nigeria>Shopping/Retail

You may contact

Olugbemisola Olabode

email: gbemiolabode@gmail.com
website: www.discoveryourgift.net

To contact the publisher:

HeartBeat Productions Inc.
Box 633
Abbotsford, BC Canada V2T 6Z8
email: heartbeatproductions@gmail.com
604.852.3761

Made in the USA
San Bernardino, CA
30 January 2017